FAITH UNDER FIRE

Betrayed By A Thing Called Love

by
LaJoyce Brookshire

Bloomington, IN   authorHOUSE   Milton Keynes, UK

AuthorHouse™
1663 Liberty Drive, Suite 200
Bloomington, IN 47403
www.authorhouse.com
Phone: 1-800-839-8640

AuthorHouse™ UK Ltd.
500 Avebury Boulevard
Central Milton Keynes, MK9 2BE
www.authorhouse.co.uk
Phone: 08001974150

First published by AuthorHouse 3/24/2006

ISBN: 1-4259-1475-6 (sc)

Library of Congress Control Number: 2006900563

Printed in the United States of America
Bloomington, Indiana

This book is printed on acid-free paper.

ADVANCE PRAISE FOR

FAITH UNDER FIRE
Betrayed by a Thing Called Love

"As, my best friend whom I totally love and so admire, LaJoyce and I have been on this journey together for a long time. To live to tell the story, to be the story, and share the story, we all are very blessed and fortunate to be a witness to God's grace and mercy and to literally see the favor on LaJoyce's life. This story can help anyone, going through anyTHING to endure their tribulation."

-Theresa Gibbs - Interior Designer,
President, SPECTACULAR STAGING
Chicago

"Thanks so much for sharing! The story is powerful and will definitely save lives. I'm so glad LaJoyce has listened to the Lord and allowed HIM to use one of her many talents in such an incredible way."

-Lencola Sullivan-Verseveldt,
Prayer Partner
The Netherlands (by way of Arkansas)

"I believe that the time is upon us where there will be a shift in power in the arenas that influence our society. God is trusting those who are sold out to HIS cause to get the attention of the masses, giving them one last chance to make a choice as to whom they will serve. Jesus is coming soon and we must take the call on our lives even more seriously because of the urgency to win souls. God is not playing and neither is the enemy. However, because we are on the winning side, we know what we must do and that we cannot be defeated if we remain willing and obedient to the leading of the HOLY SPIRIT and what he is instructing us to do. With this book, LaJoyce has followed His instructions."

-Ellie Winslow,
Make-Up Artist for the Motion Picture Industry
New York City

"A brilliant testimonial of what happens when you maintain your integrity in spite of the circumstances."

-Rev. Henzy Green, Jr.
Emaus Christian Church
Indianapolis

"I knew LaJoyce personally during this time and I didn't know from speaking with or witnessing her as she moved about that ANYTHING was wrong in her life. She is courageous and I thank her on behalf of women everywhere. How liberating this must be...not just the telling of the story, but the liberation that only complete trust and faith in God can bring."

-Terria Ladner Taylor,
Marketing Consultant
Chicago

"Wow! God's Girl For Real! This book is awesome, and extremely courageous. Sisters, we have to get free and we can only do it through truth. So much of our lives are hidden in secrets. I applaud LaJoyce for allowing God to use her to give-- if even just one woman-- the courage to be "naked and not ashamed". My sister LaJoyce has done just that."

-Evan Mykol Blake,
Film Producer
Hollywood

"When I read this, I felt the weight of the assignment for LaJoyce's life. This book is ministry. At a time when the earth is preaching the gospel, she has been given a heavy assignment and authority over a strong principality. STAND, because-- It's time."

-Theara Ward,
Praise and Professional Dancer
New York City

"I am commenting on this piece because I have a deep respect for Dr. Brookshire and I believe in the power of sharing your truth, no matter what it is, with others. I am thankful for the possibility of healing that does not limit us to always be the victim of someone else's ill intentions. I am thankful for the witness of those who have been able to move through dark experiences and have the strength to empower others by sharing how they were able to overcome them. Thanks LaJoyce for sharing your story with light and love."

-April Yvonne Garrett,
Founder/Executive Director, Civic Frame, Inc.
Baltimore

"When I read this, my heart stopped. God is so awesome and merciful to His children. I thank God for giving her the courage to share this delicate part of her life with others. Everything has a time and a season and I believe her book will inspire and help many confused and troubled women to do right by themselves and others."

-Fayette Harrington Davis,
Teacher
Atlanta

"I have known LaJoyce for years. And Wow! I had no idea the brotha put her through his "own" personal hell. He owed her the right to be honest. He took an oath and said vows on her wedding day. I guess they meant nothing to him or was he really that hateful? Or, shall I say in denial. It just goes to show, that you can't mess with God's children. He has a plan for each of us."

-Michael Hill,
WWRL Radio National/Local Sales Manager
New York City

"Thank you so much for the book that I feel I have waited all my life to read. LaJoyce is blessed with an opportunity to minister through books to millions of broken people. I must say thank you for harkening to the voice of the Lord and for being obedient. Often times we miss our destiny because our ears are not tuned to the voice of the Lord. The Word of God says that what the devil meant for bad, God meant for our good. So, "you go girl" and keep on writing books of faith, healing, and deliverance."

-Rebecca Sampson,
Avid Reader

Albany, GA

ALSO BY
LaJoyce Brookshire

Soul Food

Web of Deception

Souls of My Sisters:
Black Women Break Their Silence,
Tell Their Stories,
And Heal Their Spirits
(Contributing Essayist)

GhettOver Girls
(Contributing Essayist)

CONTENTS

INTRODUCTION

by
Debra Fraser-Howze
President/CEO
National Black Leadership Commission on AIDS

This book is the story of one African-American woman, but it is really the story or potential story of us all. One in every 50 African-American men and one in every 160 African-American women are estimated to be infected with HIV, the virus that causes AIDS according to the U.S. Centers for Disease Control and Prevention as of this writing. We are a community in the midst of a state of public health emergency, and like the victims of Katrina, we are out there all on our own.

There are some things in the history of Black people that we should never allow to be repeated, the obvious one is slavery and the other is HIV/AIDS -- but there are many, many more. In my years of service to my community and country, I have served as a presidential appointee to both the Clinton and Bush administrations, developed my own agency to help Black leaders respond to HIV/AIDS, raised millions in new funding for prevention, conducted research, developed legislation and fought for education and prevention programs at all levels and in all communities of color. We were the first to involve the Black church and leadership in a formal action plan in response to this epidemic and have conducted public policy and communality development since 1987. We have a very long way to go and HIV/

AIDS is not the last fatal disease with no cure that our community will face in the next few years -- and we are far from prepared.

But as the history of this disease is written, let it not discount the Black people who unknowingly faced imminent danger because they loved another, or those who lived in perpetual fear of this disease, or those who took the responsibility to get tested and know their status and protected themselves from a preventable infection to save both themselves, their lovers and the loved ones around them from the devastation that this disease causes.

A friend of mine, repeated a saying that has stuck with me for life. She said that one day, we will all get to heaven and before we meet our maker, we as Black people will first meet our ancestors and be made to respond to one question - - and that question is... "what did you do with your freedom?"

Based on your answer it will be determined if you used your newfound freedom to advance the cause of your people and lived your life in a way that helped others. It is a profound commentary and a question we should all live our lives in preparation to answer. We all have the freedom of free will. It takes a great deal of personal responsibility to live a life that answers this question for your family, your community, for the betterment of your people, and for yourself.

It is believed in some circles that we all come here knowing how we are going to leave and that we make this decision before we are sent. In this book several people made decisions, all of which they will be required to answer to. Make your decision the right one. LaJoyce, a beautiful, talented, young woman made a decision to honor her marriage vows and care for a dying husband with AIDS. Throughout this journey, information about the way he acquired his

HIV infection and how long he knew about it would have reshaped the thinking of any normal human being, but LaJoyce was not just any woman, she was a woman of great faith. Through this one journey in her life, which God allowed me to be a part of from its beginning to its end, I learned much about the power of love and the unimaginable power of faith. Faith in things unseen and unknown will pull you through in times when you are most in need.

What the African-American community must grapple with as we read LaJoyce's story is how we got here in the first place. While conspiracy theories abound in our community (from the white evil scientist, the government, the man-made agents, which all went awry and purposely caused the untimely death of millions of African descendents, and 40 million orphans) these theories are just one part of possible story.

When the history of HIV/AIDS in communities of African decent is written, it will be full of stories like the one LaJoyce is telling, including our collective responsibility to halt a preventable disease that kills and still has no cure.

What have you done with your freedom?

If your answer is that you did not take precautions to save your own life as an African descendent woman, and if you were a black man on the Down Low or anyone having unprotected sex and you knew there was a big disease with a little name that was sexually transmitted and took no precautions to protect your mate, then your answer to the question would have been catastrophic. The answer to how and why we got here in this thing called AIDS lay at the feet and hands of many. We are a people who have thrown caution to the wind, a society that is so racially divided that they would cut off resources from Black people that flowed in the first wave of a supposedly white epidemic when they thought they had found progress for their own; we are an advocacy community that held each other close when it was convenient and were all but abandoned when it was not; we are a government so crippled with disdain for some of its citizens that they were easily blinded into abandonment and left us to deal with a life-threatening situation - they never really told us in the beginning that we were already infected and that this would be our destruction; we are a people who went along with laws that were not in the best interest of our communities public health and, we are Black men and women who do not think ourselves worthy to stay alive, and, as this book points out, we have a group of brothers, not all but some, that are simply doing the wrong thing and putting sisters at great risk.

We can fix this!! Because Black women can fix anything!!

We can get the individual information we need by getting tested and protect all those we love, we can stop second guessing our questions about some men and deal with their real sexual issues, we can do a little more due diligence before we choose a life-long mate that will help us bear our children, we can say "you have to use a condom" no mater what our age or the environment we come from and change our attitude about ourselves to know we are worth protecting. And if all else fails, we can do what we do with our children and simply take a 'time out' until we get all the information that will keep us safe. We are not a bankrupt community and we deserve to be safe; if he says no to a condom, we are worthy enough to say good-bye.

Sistah's, you are descendents of Kings and Queens, do not let our present condition confuse you out of your royal position. Love Black men like there are no other on the face of the earth, but never allow any one of them to remove the blessing of you from the bosom of our people. Take care of yourselves- -LaJoyce did with body and soul and she continues to bless us with all she is and all the potential she has become. Walk good and walk safe, and remember…you are all potential Queens to the dynasty that is still to become Black America.

ACKNOWLEDGEMENTS

-I praise you God from whom all blessings flow, and I thank you for each and every one. I thank you Lord for giving me strength when I was weak and peace during the storm. You kept me safe and out of harm's way in order to do the task you've ordained, as this body of work has been orchestrated solely by you.

My dearest husband Gus, and Bishop of the Brookshire household, I thank you for allowing me the room to share this story so that others may be healed. From ages 12-17 you were genius in gifting me with a diary annually. You could have bought anything else with your Christmas money, but you chose a diary and that was divine. It is ironic that the art of journalizing, inspired by you, would become a favorite past-time of mine and be utilized to share these accounts with others. The conversations and turn of events that transpired during this time were accurately documented in my journals. Thank you for following your heart so that I may be able to share a piece of mine with the world - - and I do mean a piece because you have the rest! Who loves you bay-bay?!

-My sweet baby girl Brooke Angel, thank you for not typing over Mommie's pages. It is no surprise to me that you want to type every chance you get. History does repeat itself and it was a joy for me to do the same with my Grannie at 3 years old just like you. Your very own computer is on the way.

-My parents Joana & Randy Baker AKA Jo & Bo, thank you for taking a pause from all of that globetrotting to come see about your baby girl. I am eternally thankful that you had the means, the compassion, and the time to extend the love of Jesus in your hearts even when it was painful.

-My dear brothers: Randy, Jr., Brad, Lance, Craig, Dirk & Stevie thank you so much for not executing the threats, but thank you even more for your prayers. Stevie, your being here helped to remind me who we are, and whose we are.

Many thank you's are due to the valiant women and men of God, who through their ministries, my growth in the Lord has increased:

-My Pastor, Rev. William Earl Lee and his bride Evangelist Verna Lee for keeping the Word before the body of Jesus The Christ Church. And for walking in the Lord in all His ways, proving there will be no more - - absolutely no more, bad days – or nights.

-Bishop Sam Williams and family for constantly keeping me lifted in prayer. As an adopted daughter, I hope I've made you proud.

-Rev. Henzy Green, Jr. for being a shining example of how to walk with Jesus right here on earth.

-Apostle Clifford and Darlyn Turner for depositing critical nuggets in my spirit that have elevated my walk with the Lord.

-Bishop Larry and Celeste Trotter for your friendship and awesome tape ministry that travels with me world-wide.

Thanks to the following ministries that have come into my home via television and tapes providing me great comfort and enlightenment during very dark times when I couldn't get to my own house of worship:

-Trinity Broadcasting Network for being on 24-hours a day!

-Bishop Noel Jones for awakening my intellection in Jesus.

-Bishop T.D. Jakes, I know I'm a woman loosed.

-Pastor Rod Parsley for teaching me how to give up my this, for that!

-Bishop Eddie Long for teaching me how to stand during the in between.

-Bishop Ulmer, I can now say, "forward march!"

-Pastor Creflo Dollar, I've learned the importance of tithing.

-Prophetess Juanita Bynum, I now live Rapture Ready!

-Bishop Clarence McClendon, I know now that the field is the world and not just arrangements, decorations and props.

-To the team of care-givers, I hope you know how much I appreciate you:

Stacey & Claudette Dyches, Mayla Billips, Theresa Gibbs, Rev. Kenneth Pearman, Skip & Diane Anderson, Larry & Patsy Parkins and Family, Uncle Charles & Aunt Peggy and Family, Ellen Franklin, Ruth Matthews, and Nurse Tracey Sheptuk. A special thanks to Zee Dees and The Webster Family who specifically cared for me:-)

-To my Armour Bearers, Evangelist Linda McBride, Ellie Winslow, April Yvonne Garrett, Andrea Francis and Evan Mykol Blake, I am indebted to you for taking the call of coverage seriously. I continue to pray for your strength in the Lord as you keep me in prayer. Claudette Dyches (my first Armour Bearer), although you are not physically able to travel, your prayers will be received as I step onto the field of the world.

-To my team, thanks for miraculously keeping all of the balls in the air: Atty. Pamela Crockett Fish how awesome you are; Marketing Mavens Michelle Joyce Johnson, Kalima Lewis, Stacey Murray;

script writing partner Blake Roberts, publicist Gwendolyn Quinn and producer Irving Wright.

-Janine Coveney, my long-time industry sister friend, thanks for the brilliant editing! The world awaits *Blue Oasis*:-)

-Patti Caprio, the cover is awesome! You're one incredible visionary.

-To my friends who have loved me through the good and bad days, I've been able to count on your prayers when it mattered most, and that's what friends are for: Mama Brookshire, Susan Ellis, Theresa Gibbs, Faye Harrington Davis, Angela Henderson, Debbie Bryant, Lencola Sullivan- Verseveldt, Mona Lynn Wallis, Walter Briggs, E. Lynn Harris, Larry & Debra Esposito, Steve & Terri Ewing, Jimmy & Nanette Nelson, LeNardo & Olivia Nelson, Karu Daniels, Shontisha Huntley, Mike Hill, Lonai Mosley, Darwyn & Velma Ingrahm, Gordette 'Sloopy' Wilson, Pamela Avery, Dewanda Howard, Dawn Keith, Eric Dove, Kaye Cooksey, Ron & Indira Singh, Dr. Cynthia Howell, Terria Ladner Taylor, Johnetta Boone, Theara Ward, Marcenda Ry, Arlene McGruder, Maria Davis, Renee Foster, Tri Smith, LT Blassingame, and big and little "Star" Olga & Zuli Turner.

-To my National Black Leadership Commission on AIDS family - - how awesome to be in the house at the time I needed you most. Nobody but God orchestrated such an assignment. Debra Fraser-Howze, as your little sister, our lives are forever sealed as together we have experienced the deaths of Steven and, now Barron. Never has such a sad day penetrated my soul so deeply as that rainy April afternoon. Consider me always available to you, as you march in the struggle.

-Johnny Allen, Bugsy, and Vaughn Harper, I know that you too were caught in the web of deception, no hard feelings. I still love you.

-To all my Mama's on my block, down the street and around the corner in Chicago, thanks for helping to raise me.

It is my hope that I continue to be a beacon of light for the Lord.

In His Service...LaJoyce

IN MEMORY OF...

Fannie "Grannie" Hunter
Mary Celeste "Auntie" Hunter
Gus "Daddy" Brookshire, Sr.
Martha "Miss Lucille" Hubbard
Aunt Geraldine Turner
Aunt Marchita Jennings
George Howard
Barron Nathaniel Wright
The Notorious B.I.G.
Ruth Matthews
Rosa Lee Daniels
Mary Louise Daniels
Lenny Gordon
Rev. Cynthia "Ma" Vaughn
"Mama" Alma Robbins
Michael Ellis
Tim Douglas

FOREWARD

by

Brenda Stone Browder

Author

On The Up and Up:
Survival Guide for Women Living with Men on the Down Low

God has given me the opportunity to reach scores of women, connecting with their spirits to bring understanding to the Down Low phenomenon. I am amazed at the women who have found themselves in the same types of relationships as I. For years, I have truly felt as if this was only my plight. I was the only one whose husband cheated with men. This journey has enlightened me. This journey has broadened my scope of vision of this unbelievable reality.

On The Up And Up has actually enhanced my life. My friend told me to get ready for the second half of my life to be totally different from the first. Given that people do live to be 100-years-old, I am 50. From the beginning of my 50th year, things have not been the same. My relationship with Christ has deepened. I attribute this to the deliverance from all that was suffocating my growth. All of that hurt, pain and guilt from my past, has been erased.

LaJoyce like me, and the growing numbers of women who refuse to stand by silently allowing the stigmas and dangers of HIV/AIDS to continue, is sharing her story to take back the control and take back the power that HIV/AIDS has stolen in lives, relationships and family. Like Shadrach, Meshach and Abendego, she stood firm in her faith and came out of the fire victorious.

Like so many other women when she discovers she's been lied to, selfishly, and purposely placed in jeopardy, she is ready to put one hand on her hip and the other on the door handle to throw the relationship out with the trash. But instead, LaJoyce remembered her faith and chose not to take on the persona of a mad black woman. She chose to take the higher ground and stand firm in her faith. She stood by her husband until God called him home. LaJoyce stayed the course and ran the race and is now able to soar like an eagle overcoming the tests of being in an uneven relationship. LaJoyce understands, that it is not about her, but about others who lack the deep roots of her faith.

God places people together on purpose for a purpose, and it is no different with LaJoyce and I. The message remains on my voice mail today from her play brother Walter Briggs from back in 2003 with him trying to make arrangements for us to get together. He and I met coincidentally at a local festival in Ohio because he didn't want to wait in a long line to buy a pie. As I passed him my writer card he told me I should speak with his sister LaJoyce who novelized *Soul Food.*

Initially, LaJoyce and I were to speak just as writer-to-writer, but when I saw her on J.L. King's (my ex-husband) video "No More Secrets, No More Lies" discussing her deceased husband, I knew we had to get together. Finally, it was Karen Hunter who put us together and sealed our relationship as we continue this work of sharing our truths in the vineyard.

For LaJoyce to expose her life with a man who tried until his dying days to keep a secret with his fight with AIDS (as so many sadly do) because of the stigma that is attached with the disease, it is an act of heroism. She is willing to stand out before all bearing her life accepting both kudos and criticisms and continue with divine guidance to slay the stigmas.

This great literary work, *Faith Under Fire: Betrayed by a Thing Called Love* will serve those who have the privilege of reading it. Those who have had similar experiences will find solace in knowing that they are not alone. Those who have not will gain valuable information for self-empowerment. And those who are apathetic will gain understanding that turning their backs will not immunize them from HIV/AIDS touching their lives.

If not for the grace of God, there go I....

DEDICATION

For women everywhere who love and trust their men deeply.
It is my hope that before leaping into love, you take the time to
explore exactly what the container contains through prayer,
by seeking the face of God.

FAITH UNDER FIRE

Betrayed by a Thing Called Love

"But without faith, it is impossible to please Him: for he that cometh to God must believe that he is, and that he is a rewarder of them that diligently seek Him."
Hebrews 11:6

CHAPTER ONE
The Meeting

*"But seek ye first the kingdom of God and his righteousness
and all things shall be added unto you."*
Matthew 6:33

It happened quite suddenly, my falling in love. You know the kind I'm talking about - - that BAM, love-at-first-sight kind of love.

I'll never forget January 30, 1990. I was a part-time Speech teacher at the Queens Broadcasting Center, in the Jamaica section of Queens, New York. My full-time job was as writer/producer of entertainment and information programming at the Sheridan Broadcasting Networks at One Times Square Plaza in New York City.

The day before I decided to take a sick day. I cleaned off my desk, returned all phone calls and handed in the weekly scripts a day early, much to the pleasure of my executive producer.

On my "sick" day, I took a lengthy bubble bath, washed my hair, and lazed around until it was time to get to class. For some reason, I dressed carefully, in a red silk blouse, leather pants, and high heeled pumps. Quite snazzy attire for the teacher who was about to spend the next four hours correcting speech patterns for on-air hopefuls.

When I got to class, I excused myself to make copies of hand-outs when I glanced into the recording studio and saw the tallest, finest, honey-dipped colored man I had ever laid eyes on in life. I ran to the office of the director, long-time air personality Johnny Allen of New York City's KISS FM, to inquire about the eye candy I had just glimpsed.

Johnny replied, "Oh that's Steven, he's a really nice guy."

I said, "Hmmm, Steven. I have a brother named Stephen." While at the copier I took another long look at the honey-dip, giving him brownie points on name alone before returning to my class.

When saying our good byes for the evening, Johnny introduced me to Steven and I turned as red as my blouse due to his charming demeanor. Johnny announced that he had arranged for Steven to take me home.

"Take me home, all the way to Brooklyn?" was my question, as we were in Queens. A 45-minute train ride and easily an hour-plus drive away.

"I'll take you all the way to Pennsylvania if that's where you live," was Steven's reply.

I raised an is-this-guy-for-real eyebrow at Johnny and he winked a sign of approval.

"Let's roll," I said, gathering my things.

On the ride home we exchanged regular pleasantries, asked typical questions and laughed a lot. He kept thanking God. I liked that part. Coming from a Baptist born-and-bred background, God is indeed at the top of my list.

"Why do you keep saying, 'Thank you God'?" I asked.

"I wasn't even supposed to be at the school tonight. I missed my final because I was in the hospital and I had to complete it tonight. So I'm saying 'thank you God' because I wouldn't have met you if I had not been in the hospital."

The reporter in me piqued, "Why were you in the hospital?"

"Bleeding ulcers."

I contorted my face. "Bleeding ulcers!?" I asked unbelievably, "How old are you?"

"Thirty-one," he answered. "I've just had a lot of problems, a bad marriage, and lots of stress on my job. But now that I've met you, all of that is about to change."

We continued with pleasant conversation and got lost trying to get to Brooklyn from Queens. The only way he knew how to get us out of the circle we seemed to be spinning around in was to go all the way to Manhattan and then back to Brooklyn. Our one-hour ride turned into three hours with traffic.

At my front door we exchanged numbers and he waited at his car to see that I had made it safely into my apartment. I looked out of the window to wave and he was leaning against his car looking up at my window. He acknowledged my wave with a beep of his automatic car alarm. As much as I hated to admit it, I was soaring from being in Steven's company.

The next day at work in the studio, we were playing radio station WBLS while making preparations for our weekly syndicated production, when deejay Bugsy announced, "Here is 'Ready or Not' by After 7 for LaJoyce Hunter from Steven. He wants her to know that he's coming for her ready or not."

My office mates and I screamed and my phone started ringing off the hook. Everyone wanted to know who this Steven was. My reply was the same: "Some dude I met yesterday!"

Being in the radio and record business had some advantages and one of them was access to the hotline number in the dee-jay booth at WBLS, the other was knowing Bugsy personally. After fielding phone calls from friends I called Bugsy myself to inquire how in the world this Steven managed to get him to make such a declaration before AND after the song played.

Bugsy said, "I know Steven, too, because of him being a part-time producer with Vaughn Harper's Quiet Storm radio program for Japan." Vaughn Harper was the premiere night-time "voice" in New York and was like a father to me in the business. Bugsy and I had always been really friendly with one another and he was like a big brother.

He issued his stamp of approval: "Now Steven is someone I'd really like to see you with. I can vouch for him all the way."

"Really," I said, knowing that Bugsy had shared his disdain for the guy I had dated in the past from the station.

"Yep. Really," he said knowingly of the other situation.

"Thanks Bugs. I'll keep you posted."

Later that afternoon, a delivery man brought two dozen, red long-stemmed American Beauties from Steven. This guy was really pouring it on and I loved it!

I phoned to thank him for the roses and the dedication and he invited me to dinner the following evening. We went to a very pricey restaurant on the East River and we both had lobster and champagne. He had another dozen roses at the restaurant for me, as he said, "to keep at home." The others were for me to keep at my office.

36

Steven romanced me with dinners in expensive restaurants at least twice a week. As a producer of entertainment programming, I always had tickets to concerts, plays or new movies in town. My responsibilities kept me out at least three nights a week. We always got two tickets to an event so Steven became my new "hot date." Him taking me to dinners was his way of controlling some of our outings since it was a given that we would attend any event for free. We were going out five nights a week!

For the first three months of our dating, Steven had roses delivered to my job every week until I told him to stop. It was established early on that we were both definitely in love. Like I said, it was that-love-at-first-sight kind of love. It was all signed, sealed and delivered by the time we had sex, intensifying the blush of our new love.

Steven further locked in the relationship by introducing me to his mother and two sisters. They all lived in the family home in Lakeview, New York, a predominantly black middle-class Long Island town. We all got along extremely well and his older sister and I could pass for sisters. We both have that *café con leche* (with lots of *leche*), light-brown-eyes, and sandy hair thing going on. When we went out together people always asked us if we were sisters and we'd just laugh and say "yes!"

We did a lot of flaunting one another in front of our friends. It was mutual that there was nothing but love between us all. Steven's best friend Stacey and his wife Claudette were the best of our buddies. They are one crazy pair. We'd go to midnight bowling almost every weekend and win all of the prizes because they played games with guessing the musical artists. Yeah, right. I only ate, and slept music as a career for the last I-don't-know-how many years, so winning was a shoo-in. We discussed many times if it was even fair for me to play because I was in the entertainment business, but we'd just shrug and collect our prizes. The real superstar of that game was Claudette. We dubbed that girl "the-foremost-knowledgeable-person-about-information-that-don't-mean-s-h-i-t." She needed to be a contestant on pop-culture trivia shows and I guarantee you, she would be the winner. To this day Claudette and Stacey are permanent fixtures in my life.

Steven and I were spending so much time together every night doing my job so I could write and keep the nation entertained, that he had a hard time getting himself to his job at Bayside BMW where he was the assistant parts manager. He had practically moved into my Brooklyn apartment. I refused to say that he "lived" there. That was against my religion. I wasn't playing house with anyone. Plus - - my Mommie would kill me!

It was easier for him to bring a bag with his stuff in it every week for whatever we would be attending and leave for work from there. He definitely tried to move in on me. I would take his clothes out of the closet that he'd leave hanging there and pack them for him and I refused to give him space in my drawer. Call me old-fashioned, but it was bad enough that I was sleeping with this dude and he wasn't my husband. Yes, I knew better.

At the time, I had a male roommate named Derrick. Now, his girlfriend Tina "lived" with us. They met at Columbia University. Derrick was an awesome budding attorney at one of the top law firms in mid-town Manhattan and Tina was an accountant. We needed to share the apartment because neither of us could afford the rent alone for the magnificent two-bedroom, two bathroom apartment in Brooklyn's Clinton Hill section. Our rent was twelve hundred dollars in 1989! Steven offered to help pay my rent, but I flatly refused.

By December 1, 1990 –just eleven months after our first meeting - we were married. The ride to the altar was rocky, as was all that followed the wedding. Here is my real-life tale of a woman betrayed by a thing called love, of putting my Faith under Fire. Read on and learn…

CHAPTER TWO

The Wedding

"...he who finds a wife, findeth a good thing"
Proverbs 18:22

One Sunday evening in June 1990 at Steven's home, we were having champagne in his sister's room watching movies. When I got to the bottom of my glass I almost swallowed a diamond ring! The whole family knew about his plan and when I screamed, everyone came in the room to offer congratulations.

We got out the calendar and immediately began looking for the best dates to get married. With his mother's insistence, we chose December 1st. Wow, less than six months away! We had work to do - - and a lot of it. My hometown is Chicago and a girl just *had* to get married in the bride's hometown, at least that's what Emily Post says.

In my opinion, the first thing we needed to do was to get ourselves a budget and stick to it. When we started analyzing our finances I discovered that Steven was $30,000 in debt!

"Steven you've got to stop using your credit cards now, or we'll never get married. How did you get this much in debt?"

"Well, I put new windows on the house for my mother, you know I like to wear nice clothes. Our dinners, the roses..."

My head was spinning. All of those dinners and roses and nice clothes contributed to this mass of debt? Yes, he did love to dress well and he shopped in places like Saks Fifth Avenue, Macy's, Nordstrom's and small boutiques. He had recently bought a line of new outfits so that he could hang out with me, he said. I saw that one price tag was $550 for a matching sweater, turtleneck and pants outfit.

"You're done," I told him. "No more roses, no more dinners, no more five-hundred-dollar outfits. You're done. From this day forward, you're on a budget. I don't want to get married and be under all of this debt. Maybe we should wait to get married until you can clear up most of it."

His mother heard me say this to him and interjected that she would help him pay down his debt. "It's hard to find true love," she said. "Don't let money stop you from getting married. Most people would never get married if they waited until they had the money. I'll help him. Will your parents help you with your debt?"

"My debt?" I asked as I showed her the worksheet I'd created. "I only have six hundred and fifty dollars worth of rent and utilities. My Grannie taught me to use cash. And while I like to shop I have never spent five hundred and fifty dollars on any one outfit and I doubt if I ever will."

When I met Steven, I was planning to leave New York by year's end. I believed the cliché if you make it in New York you can make it anywhere. My goal was to work for six years in New York City, save my money, go back to Chicago, buy a four to six family rental unit, move back into my room at Mommie's house and become a real estate mogul in addition to writing entertainment shows.

The differences in our financial views on that day of engagement were very clear. Instead of us celebrating, we spent the rest of the evening writing budgets with his mother until it was time for her to get to her nursing job at Mercy Hospital.

She left us that evening with one thought I'll never forget: "There's nothing wrong with buying nice clothes and having nice things, LaJoyce. Steven is accustomed to really nice things."

I thought out loud, "Yeah, but at whose expense? Now that Steven was going to get married, his spending habits needed to change." The South Side of Chicago versus the Long Island upbringing conflicts were in full swing!

Steven's mother insisted that I call her Mom. Her name was Mozelle, so I dubbed her Mama Mo. My Mommie's name is Joana and many of her friends call her Jo, and my Daddy's name is Bo. So we had Mo, Jo and Bo. They were too many things already and they hadn't even met yet.

Now that we were engaged, I gave Steven a card one evening that read:*"You've found the key to my happiness without my having to tell you. You've found the key to my laughter without my having to tell you. You've found the key to my love without my having to tell you. The key that I do want to give to you, is the one to my house."*

Then I handed him a key to my apartment. He was speechless! He was always there after he had carte blanche access. He had practically moved in then.

My girlfriend from high school, Kaye, who was a flight attendant based out of LaGuardia airport for six months, was forced to sleep in the window seat because of his constantly spending the night. I felt guilty, but she insisted she didn't mind.

The one thing that we had to do immediately was go to Chicago so that he could meet my family and see where and how I was raised. I had already called several hotels and made appointments for viewing for the wedding to take place that December.

We drove into Chicago in July and upon our arrival at 4 a.m., Steven wanted to check into a local motel and sleep before going to my house. I flatly refused, because my father knew what time we left and would be worried if we didn't show up at the appointed hour. The motel he wanted to check into was a flea-bag one on Stony Island Avenue!

"You don't roll into Chicago, honey, and check into the wrong motel at 4 a.m. when a girl's father is waiting for her to show up. You do New York and your people, let *me* navigate Chicago."

"But, I want to snuggle with you tonight," he cried. "I'm not going to be able to sleep in the same bed with you the whole time we're here."

"You got that right. You'll survive," I told him. "We're here for you to meet my parents, my friends and to find a place for a wedding. You can get your butt rubbed back at home. You will have to wait."

This conversation spun out of control into our first huge argument. He ranted like a three-year-old who couldn't get his way, "But I'm tired. I need a shower. I want to be fresh when I meet your mother. I'm cranky. I'm horny. And I want to sleep until I'm ready to wake up."

I didn't listen and when I got tired of arguing with him I simply drove up in front of the house and got out of the car. My father opened the door and said, "Right on time!"

I threw Steven a knowing look that said, "See."

At 9 a.m. my best-friend-in-the-whole-wide-world, Theresa, whom I lovingly call Tyger, bounded into the house full of energy to scoop me up so I could go out with her to talk. But first, she went to the guest room to check out the sleeping fiancé. I thought she was going to just tip to peek at him, but when she flipped on the light to get a good look he woke up. I heard them speaking but I didn't know what they were discussing.

It wasn't until years later that Tyger told me he cussed her out. I was floored. She knew better than to tell me that crap then, because he would have been an ex-fiancé before he even got the chance to say good morning to my mama. Knowing me the way a best-friend-in-the-whole-wide-world should know you, she decided not to tell me.

This is also why I brought him home. I needed to know if Steven could play well with others. If I bring someone home to pass the Crest Test, you should let me know if they fail! Cussing out my best friend equals failure.

We left him sleeping and I returned two hours later to find him getting dressed to meet the folks. He was laboring over what to wear.

"Put on your sweats," I said, "It's my mama, not some industry party."

"Are you kidding! I'm meeting your mother for the first time, I have to come correct."

"Believe me, she won't be judging your outfit. Hurry up, breakfast is on the stove."

When he came down, he was decked out in a three-piece matching outfit with gold jewelry on his neck, wrists and fingers. At 11 a.m. he looked like he was ready for an evening out. My mama was still in her robe and as I speculated, my parents never said a word about what he was wearing. Steven charmed them as only he could best and my parents were hooked.

Due to the within-six-months date of our wedding, all of the hotels in town kept referring me to the Guest Quarter Suites Hotel on North Michigan Avenue that was under construction. Mommie, Steven and me went downtown for a tour. When the catering director handed us hard hats, we were surprised. Only the first two floors and the top two floors were completed. The ballroom in which we were to have our wedding was not completely finished either. The good thing was, since we were standing in an incomplete hotel wearing a hard hat and had no real samplings of what the room would look and feel like, not to mention there being no food to taste, the price of the wedding for 250 people was quite reasonable. My Mommie's face lit up like a Christmas tree.

During the rest of our visit, friends and family flooded the house to meet the husband-to-be. He was showered with hugs, warm welcomes and lots of hushed corner conversations. It seemed as if Steven was passing the Crest Test from my people and I was very happy.

One friend from Indianapolis, Henzy, told me when we hugged that he sensed another presence around me and that Steven and I must be very close. Henzy and I had been long time friends, business partners and spiritual prayer warriors since the mid-1980s. I valued and trusted his spiritual discernment and wisdom.

In Long Island, Steven was in the habit of driving me around to neighborhoods and showing me the homes of the girls' houses where he had, "gotten the panties." This was an awesome conquest for him to have run through the entire neighborhood, and he was proud of it.

While in Chicago he asked me, "Where are some of your old boyfriends houses?"

"I've only had two boyfriends here, but I'll drive you by Gus' house first."

Why he wanted to see an old boyfriend's home, I'll never know. I drove up in front of the house. "There it is!" I announced. Steven knew the whole story with me and Gus. We were boyfriend and girlfriend from age 12 to 17, with several break-ups along the way. Gus was definitely my first true love. We promised ourselves that we'd get married sometime after college when we had a chance to experience life. Gus joined the Air Force and moved to Texas and I moved to New York. In 1989, Gus called me one night to announce his engagement. I cried my eyes out, wrote him a tear-stained letter but told myself, it was time to find myself a husband too. One year later, here I was with my fiancé in front of Gus' house. *Nah, nah.*

Steven was admiring their flowers in the yard when we heard a knock-knock on the hood of the car. There was Gus! I threw the car in park, Gus grabbed me out and swung me around in the street. We stood there hugging and screaming in our surreal moment.

Mama Brookshire came to Steven's rescue with a hug, "I'm Mama, oh, you must be Steven. Well we've heard so much about you. Just park the car honey. That's her brother, don't mind them. You come on inside."

He did as he was told while Gus and I bounced into the house, arm in arm. We visited for about an hour and excused ourselves, because we were on a tight schedule.

In the car Steven stated, "I don't know why you didn't get married to Gus."

"He married someone else and that's all there was to it."

"But you've gotta ask YOURself, why?"

The way he said it was such a failed attempt to dig at my self-esteem, that I turned the car around the corner and drove back in front of Gus' house. "Get out of the car, YOU ask him!"

He started stuttering.

"Yeah, that's what I thought. Aren't you glad he didn't marry me so you could?"

"Yes, I am," he admitted and kissed me to seal the deal and as an apology.

Back in New York, I had an August weekend fete for my bridesmaids to meet the designer Franklin Rowe so he could create their gowns for the wedding. Mommie flew in for the occasion and to meet Mama Mo. Franklin was the most awesome designer of the day and I had several knock-out pieces from him. For our December wedding, the color scheme was emerald green and ivory velvet. I was wearing an ivory beaded bodice with an ivory velvet skirt. The whole idea was to have this gorgeous beaded top to wear later with ivory pants, and a slimming skirt in both velvet and satin.

Mommie and Mama Mo, whom we dubbed Mo and Jo, hit it off immediately. Upon their first introduction they were giggling like little kids as they jumped in the car and headed to the mall in search of the perfect color for them both. They decided to wear the same color, same material but different style dresses. At the mall they would choose which color and material looked best. Jo and Mo were gone for so long we started to worry.

When they returned, well after dark, I told Steven, "Well, they could have come back in an hour saying, 'I can't stand that woman.' Shopping together for a full eight hours, means they love each other."

Steven was wearing an ivory brocade blazer, with velvet pants. Being the fashionista he was, he wanted to have a second blazer made to change into at the reception, which was half brocade and half velvet. I had to admit that it was incredibly sharp. His garments were going to cost more than mine. I reminded him that he was over our wedding budget and his personal budget by getting two jackets.

"It's our wedding, don't you want me to be sharp?" he whined.

"Yeah," I said, but thinking, *he can't give Franklin a credit card.* My additional items to go with my gown weren't going to be made until after the wedding and not until I needed them and could afford them. Like I mentioned, I had several Franklin Rowe originals and they weren't cheap. I'd known Franklin about six years and I bought one item annually. At that very moment, cheap is what I was accused of being.

I wanted the girls to be in emerald green velvet suits, with rhinestone buttons. But each of the girls' dresses would be different to reflect their personalities. I was a victim of the "closet full of ugly bridesmaids dresses" syndrome and I vowed it would end with me. I wanted their dresses to be a take-away item to wear again and again.

Mommie and my girls Pam, Lencola, Tyger, Mayla, Mama Mo and Steven's two sisters crowded into my apartment for an afternoon with Franklin. He sat back and watched us engage with one another for hours and one by one he called the girls over to him. He was sketching each girl based on what he had observed. All of them let out a squeal of delight at what he had done and he proceeded to take their measurements. The designs were awesome. No one was disappointed.

Fuschia was their color of choice for the Moms and satin was the material. Both of them stood at 5 feet two and Franklin came up with exquisite designs.

The designs were underway, the hotel was selected and I was getting married. Weeeeee dawgie, we were gonna have a wedding!

It was time for me to renew the lease on my apartment but Steven and his mother came up with the bright idea to have me move into a room in their house to save money for our new apartment until the wedding. I protested at first because the extra room was currently for family storage. We made a big party out of cleaning it out, which took every bit of an entire weekend for it to be cleaned and organized.

When I moved in Mama Mo had one rule: Steven was not allowed to sleep in my room. I agreed that would be the proper thing to do. Steven protested to the point of a full argument with his mom. I was shocked that he didn't see such an act as disrespectful in his mother's home. The other rules were general good room-mate considerations - clean-up behind yourself, don't hog the bathroom, take a message if someone calls.

I was easy in the kitchen department since I didn't eat the kinds of foods they ate. They were one carnivorous family! I didn't and still don't eat red meat. Instead I eat lots of raw foods, fruits and nuts. They dubbed me "Rabbit" and I don't know who started it first, but Steven called me that all of the time. I always told them eating right, going to bed early, taking dance classes and a long walk would keep me looking young forever. They would make fun of my garbage salads complete with red cabbage (yum) and my 9 p.m. bedtime all they wanted, but I'm the first one sleepy in the bunch.

PolyGram Records had a Las Vegas night for one of their artists and it was set up just like a real casino. They issued tickets for various prizes and the grand prize was a trip to the Bahamas. Steven was a big winner earning lots of tickets and of course jockeying for the Bahamas trip. Everyone there rallied around us. Several of my industry friends collected tickets from others so that we would have the most.

"Give them your tickets," they shouted, "they're getting married!"

Sure enough we won the Bahamas trip. Everyone was very happy for us. It was like having an un-official engagement party.

We took the Bahamian trip over the Labor Day weekend. Steven was angry about the accommodations which consisted of a basic Howard Johnson type room. Two steps up from a dive. He wanted to check out and go to a luxury resort. I was not in the mood to have an argument, but I had to continue to be sagacious for the sake of our financial future.

"All we have to do is sleep in here Steven, let's just go and enjoy the Bahamas. Can't you stay focused. We're going on a Hawaiian honeymoon. This trip didn't cost us a dime."

"We do have to pay for food."

"And because you like to eat in five-star restaurants that will cost us more than this trip cost PolyGram. Let's have some good meals reasonably priced, some good beach, and stay right here. It's only four days."

He reluctantly did stay but not without constant reminders every time we came into the room, and he would pout himself to sleep. I wasn't feeling too well, and I chalked it up to the rush-rush of the trip, the wedding planning, and the move. It was on this trip that I learned to pay Steven no mind at all. My natural father, Duke taught me one very valuable lesson: "Don't try to be logical with illogical people."

When we got back home I made the most awesome discovery: I was pregnant! At 28, here I was getting married to my dream man and about to have a baby. I'd be only five months pregnant walking down the aisle and that would be fine with me. So, Henzy *was* right, the other presence he sensed around me was a baby!

Steven had quite a different reaction. He wanted us to keep it hush-hush. He said it wasn't a good idea to tell people you were pregnant before three months. I had heard that somewhere, so I agreed. I told no one.

One week later, he told me that he wasn't ready to start a family right away and that he wanted me to have an abortion so that we could start out right. He lamented over the relationship with his first wife, who already had a toddler when they got married and it was very hard for them to get established with a "crumb snatcher" in tow.

I told him he was nuts. Just like his mother said we should not wait on money to get married, I thought we should not toss out the baby because of money. We'd make it if he wanted to make it.

"Think about it very carefully," I suggested as I bounced off to take my evening walk.

The next Saturday morning, Steven woke me up at 6:00 a.m. fully dressed in a suit, "Get dressed," he said.

I didn't know where we were going so I put on a dress, stockings and pumps. We drove deeper into Long Island and he pulled up to a nondescript office building.

When we got inside I could clearly see this was a doctor's office. He gave my name at the window and they handed him some papers which he gave to me saying, "I've thought about it. I don't want to start off with a baby."

Whaaaaaat! I screamed in my head. That black girl south-side-of-Chicago thing jumped out, "Since it takes two to raise a baby, if you don't want your baby then neither do I."

I snatched the papers and sat down to complete them. They called my name and off I went – to get an abortion. It was definitely a surreal experience. I had talked about women who had abortions, and I didn't think I'd find myself in this predicament. Lesson learned - - never say never. All I remember is the doctor - who was bottled-blonde with her glistening one-carat diamond studs in each ear - between my legs.

When I entered the waiting room expecting to see Steven, he wasn't there. I went in the parking lot to look for the car, he wasn't there. I wanted and needed to lay down, but I had to settle for the waiting room until he returned. If I still had my apartment, I would have headed home to my own bed at that moment. Oddly, I didn't have any regrets about the abortion. My mother raised me without my father Duke, until Bo Daddy came along my senior year of high school. And while she never complained my brother Stevie and I never suffered, but I wanted to do it differently.

I should have been sitting there viewing Steven differently. Instead I pulled out my wedding check-list and went over it in the lobby until he returned some 45 minutes later.

"Are you OK?" was all he could manage.

"No, are you OK? Mission accomplished, baby is gone. You satisfied?"

He avoided the question and asked, "You want to get something to eat?"

"I want to lay down."

"Can we get something right quick? I'm starving."

"What have you been doing for the last five hours?"

"I went to the mall, walked around, and went to the movies."

"I just unexpectedly walked into an office building with a baby, now I'm walking out minus one, and you took your ass to the movies?"

I'm not the cussing type because I have lots and lots of words. In fact he accused me of using vocabulary words he didn't understand just to confuse him. He clearly understood that.

"What else was I going to do all this time?" he whined, trying to assuage my brewing temper.

"Wait! Anything could have gone wrong."

"Daaaag, where's your faith?"

"Don't you dare bring God into this conversation that way. I need to lay down."

He turned the car off and was opening the car door for me. I hadn't noticed we were in the parking lot of his favorite steak house. Not only did he not wait, but now he was taking me to a steak house when he knew I didn't eat red meat!

Pissed off wasn't even the word. I looked at what I was doing and couldn't believe love had just run off with my heart and my head like that. I was in love with this man down to my core, it was just that simple.

Back at home I climbed into my pajamas and onto the couch in the living room. Mama Mo kept coming down finding things to discuss with me. I'd give her short answers because I wasn't much in the mood for talking. I finally asked Steven what he'd bought since he was at the mall for five hours. He said he purchased things to take on the honeymoon.

Mama Mo made the announcement that night about our honeymoon to Hawaii.

"I will be sending you guys on a 15-day, all-inclusive, five-star honeymoon to Hawaii as your wedding gift."

Steven jumped up and hugged her.

"Thank you," I said. "Hawaii is a very expensive place, and 15 days is a very long time to be away. You don't have to put us up in five-star hotels."

"Oh yes I do," she said adamantly. "Steven deserves some happiness and I just want to help to make him happy. He's always wanted to go to Hawaii."

Since I had been managing our money, I knew Steven did not have any extra dollars laying around to pay for an abortion. Mama Mo *had* to be the one to pay for it! It was so in my face at that moment. Her sitting there telling me about her baby boy's happiness and my lying there with an empty womb. The juxtaposition of that one almost threw me off the couch.

Lord, please help me from slapping them both right here, I prayed to myself. But I said, "Amen" aloud.

"That's right, Amen," Mama Mo said, figuring I was co-signing her statement about Steven's happiness. "Then it's settled, 15 days in Hawaii it is!"

I went to bed asking the Lord's forgiveness for what I'd done that day. I also asked him not to punish me by never letting me have a child in the future. I know how He is a forgiving God. I know He had mercy on me. Mercy is something given to you because you don't deserve to have it, an unrestrained exercise of authority, if you will. That song we used to sing at my church in Chicago came flooding back and I whispered the words and fell into a deep sleep: *"...When I fall on my knees, with my face to the rising sun. Oh Lord have mercy on me."*

My Mommie called me at work to say that Mama Mo called her to ask if she and Daddy Bo would pay five-thousand dollars for us to stay in Hawaii an additional five days.

"Heckie nooooo! I told her LaJoyce has been all over the world, they can go back to Hawaii on their own dime if they like it that much," Mommie said. "I have a wedding to pay for."

Mama Mo told her that she was cashing in fifteen-thousand dollars of her deceased husband's pension just so we could thoroughly enjoy ourselves and because we would never have this opportunity again.

"I told that woman you would just have to enjoy yourself in 15 days and that's long enough to be honeymooning anyway!"

My Mommie is not the one. She takes no tea for the fever. I could only imagine how this conversation really sounded with loud booming "No Ma'am's." That's my mama!! : -)

My girlfriends in New York showed up in full force for my bridal shower at our new Brooklyn apartment in Fort Greene. Steven wanted to stay so badly, but it just wasn't right for the groom to be lurking around the women's festivities. He just knew there'd be a stripper. I was disappointed to know he saw me as a stripper kind of girl. My friends know that I'm not, so of course there was none.

Everyone brought their signature dish and it was on! The fellowship, the prayers, the gifts - - oh, my, my, the gifts! One friend just said aloud, "LaJoyce, you're truly blessed!"

"Yes, I am," I said through tears.

I had been a co-host of at cable television program called "Woman of the Week" for several years and the executive producer, Miss Lucille, was like a surrogate mother to me. She wanted me feted with her friends who knew me in "Miss Lucille" style. She was a grand diva with a tremendous amount of style and class. Her gathering was at A Dish of Salt, one of New York City's premiere Chinese food restaurants. Those ladies sent me off with gifts I'd have never considered. Miss Lucille beamed at the success of her party for me. I was humbled and thankful.

Our arrival in Chicago was met with an incredible amount of fanfare from family and friends. The flurry of airport (Midway and O'Hare), Greyhound, and Amtrak arrivals had forced our calendars into a well-coordinated frenzy. Steven and I still had business to take care of at the Cook County Clerk's Office with the marriage license.

Right there in the County Clerk's office, I almost walked off from this dude when he tried to force me into having his name on the license without a hyphenation. That's when I flipped out.

I told that clerk, "You put LaJoyce Hunter and a hyphen before that name."

"I thought you were really ready to get married. I thought you were old-fashioned," he questioned, trying to lay a guilt trip on me in front of the clerk. Steven had been like a knight-in-shining-armor, rescuing me from my single status at age twenty-eight. I was dangerously in love and ready for a husband and he knew it.

"I'm both ready to get married and old-fashioned but I will never give up my name totally. I will, however, add yours. Or," I said standing my ground in my hometown, "we don't have to do this."

The sister-friend-clerk looked over her glasses at him for his answer and he just said, "do whatever you want."

I repeated myself firmly to the clerk, "LaJoyce Hunter hyphen."

And that, was the end of that.

Our rehearsal at Saint John Church-Baptist was flawless. Tyger was the wedding coordinator and she did a bang-up job. It was surreal being in the same church about to be married by Pastor Johnson who Christened, baptized, and debutanted me. I sat on the steps leading to the altar watching the rehearsal. It was in this very church I went to Sunday School, sang in the choir with my first solo, had my first communion, received my first Bible, got my first college scholarship and spoke from the pulpit. There was a lot of history for me oozing in those walls. I was about to make another indelible St. John's imprint in my mind in less than 24 hours and I was getting nervous.

The rehearsal dinner was held at my mother's house and the food was prepared by her best friend, who I called Aunt Marchita. She cooked my favorite meal, turkey and dressing with a stuffed red snapper. It was just the best-ever festive fellowship. I was pleased to have my two favorite students, Shontisha and Karu make the journey from New York. Neither of them had ever traveled out of state before and they had a great time enjoying my family.

My best friend-in-the-whole-wide-world,Tyger along with my high school buddy and former New York roommate Kaye gave me a slam-dunk lingerie bridal shower. Oh, the champagne, the lovely lingerie, and to my surprise a stripper named Tiger! Only Tyger could have dug up such a thing. My friends were so shocked at his appearance that he didn't even have to bother me!

My Bo Daddy woke me up to advise me it was December 1st, my wedding day, and his calendar said I needed to get to the hair dresser. I was so groggy and fuzzy, probably from too much champagne. Definitely from nervousness.

He first had to drive me to Walgreen's where I bought Pepto-Bismol for the first time in my life and drank it right out of the bottle at the counter to ease my queasiness.

Super-star hair stylist Davvy did the honors at her shop and I was literally listless as she navigated me from station to station. I kept swigging my bottle of Pepto-Bismol and I prayed that this feeling in my stomach would pass. I don't know how much time went by, but my Bo Daddy was standing before me as Davvy was flinging off the vinyl cover-up. My hair was glued into an awesome up-do that would not come un-done unless I washed it.

By the time I got home, I had semi-snapped out of my morning haze. Good thing I was all better, because it was sheer bedlam at my house! I gathered all of my things and whispered to Bo Daddy, "Take me to the church."

"Now? So early?" he questioned since the wedding was at 4 p.m.

I looked around at the chaos, "Now."

The janitor, whom I've known him since I was a kid, was just unlocking the church said, "Now baby, why you the first one here? Ain't never known no bride to be the first one here."

"I had to leave my house."

"Come on baby, let's go to your dressing room."

There was a peace that enveloped me sitting all alone in the church where my spiritual foundation was actually built. I felt home, loved, safe. I cuddled myself up in an old, huge, red velvet pulpit chair in the room and went soundly to sleep for more than an hour.

When I woke up, I immediately went to work on my face. The dramatics of Davvy's up-do and Franklin's gown called for my face to be beat - - totally beat, replete with lashes. During my makeup application, I kept telling myself not to cry. "You better not ruin this makeup job, girl. It has to last you through the night."

With my makeup, hair and nap done, I sat in my velvet chair and awaited the arrival of my bridesmaids. They each arrived rushed and to some extent un-done. Their gifts from me were dangling rhinestone earrings with a tiny ball on the end. I had discussed my vision of them wearing up-do's so it could show off their necklines with those earrings. But who showed with an up-do? Only Tyger and my prayer partner Lencola. So I had to comb the hair of my cousin Mayla, Pam, and Steven's two sisters.

Growing up doing dance shows and fashion shows, I have always been resident face painter, and my wedding day was no different. So I had to beat Tyger, Mayla and Steven's two sisters.

Meanwhile, we got the word that the limo never showed at the hotel for Steven and his crew. Everyone started offering to do this and that.

I didn't even look up. "Tell them to get a cab. The hotel is on North Michigan Avenue, this church is South Michigan Avenue - - same street. They'll be here in less than 15 minutes."

Everyone exhaled, I kept making-up my girl.

My early arrival to the church got me centered, calm, rested and un-affected by the wedding brouhaha that seems to stir just before it begins. I hadn't prayed that the day be OK, I prayed that I be OK. Ultimately, I knew only God would be in control of the day.

I did not step into my dress until I was absolutely sure we were about to begin. I didn't want not one crease in my velvet skirt. We were all flawless! The emerald and ivory velvet with the rhinestone accents shimmered. Mommie and Mama Mo were as beautiful as could be in their fuchsia. My Grannie was beaming and draped with fur and pearls, and Steven's Godmother Martha had come all the way from Los Angeles. It was a perfect production.

We made a circle and I asked Lencola to pray. We had been prayer partners for many years, praying on the phone each morning at 7 a.m. It was only fitting that she bring the group prayer. And pray she did which sealed the presence of the Holy Spirit and a sense of calm to all in the room. I looked at her and winked.

The girls were walking down the aisle to the immaculate voice of my friend from church, Ella, singing Anita Baker's "You Bring Me Joy."

Bo Daddy and I were waiting in the back of the church when I told him, "I've got the strangest feeling I shouldn't be doing this."

He unwrapped my arm from his. "Who we got to tell!?" he said in his daddy-protect-daughter haughtiness. "Who we got to tell!? See, we can go downtown, have ourselves a party with all that food there, and then I'll take you to Hawaii my damn self!"

"I'm just nervous, c'mon," I recanted, grabbing his arm.

"Yeah, I got your nervous," he said looking at me sideways.

Just then I saw my sister friend Janine and her husband from New York run into the sanctuary to get a seat. They were a solid couple who had endured their share of bumps and curves, but they'd made it. Seeing them helped my calm return and we stepped to the doorway. I honestly had to gasp at the loveliness of the church all aglow with candle light, emerald, ivory, and rhinestones. I knew a lot of people were trying to make it from New York but I didn't know how many. I was moved to see my new friends there.

My girl Davette arranged to take the LSAT's that day in Chicago just so she could be there, but didn't know if she'd be finished in time to get to the church. When I saw her, I said aloud, "You made it!" Everyone laughed. I knew the mental gymnastics involved in taking such an exam, and her finishing early meant good bye record business, hello law school. She had made it in more ways than one.

I saw Steven put on his glasses so he could see me better because he couldn't see from long distances. I had told him not to miss the main event - - my walking down the aisle. I'd also told him not to cry because that would make me cry. I didn't want an hour's plus make-up job on the front of my beaded bodice. Call me vain, but I wanted pretty pictures!

They would absolutely be pretty pictures because Steven looked FINE in his brocade and velvet jacket. So did the ushers. I hoped my single girlfriends didn't bring sand to the beach. Stacey was Steven's best man and he was struggling not to cry. He kept inhaling deeply and holding his eyes wide open.

Pastor Johnson asked, "Who gives this bride...?"

Bo Daddy had his chest all puffed out, "I do!" Everyone rolled.

Lencola stepped out of the bridesmaid's line to sing the "Lord's Prayer." That girl gave the church goosebumps. Her voice soared all up into the rafters of Saint John Church-Baptist and hung out there for the duration of the service.

"Dearly Beloved, We are gathered here today..." began Pastor Johnson. When he got to the vows part, that's when I felt as if I'd cry. I held back until I said, "in sickness and in health." A single crocodile tear rolled down my right cheek and underneath my chin. Steven's eyes welled-up and I shook my head one time and squeezed his hand for him to hold on.

We made it through with no crying and off to the reception. The Guest Quarter Suites had literally decked the halls for Christmas. It was all so festive; the tone was set.

We danced our first dance to Babyface's "Sunshine," that was also an alternative nickname for me other than Rabbit. While we were dancing, Steve ordered the DJ, my Uncle Johnny, to play a serious jam.

"I got it," Uncle Johnny said.

"I mean is that a serious jam?" Steven asked craning his neck to see the title of what was on the secondary turntable.

Uncle Johnny is a seasoned Chicagoland DJ. "Man, I got it."

The song strummed two beats and everyone there – at least everyone from Chicago - screamed and jumped out of their seats and headed to the dance floor. The 1976 dusty, "Love's Gonna Last" by Jeffery was the song and so appropriate for a first jam song for the crowd. It is a beloved stepper's cut in Chicago and one to guarantee the announcement that a party was now underway.

Well, Mr. New York DJ Steven had never heard this song before and he went straight off! I mean he went up to Uncle Johnny and was ordering him to take off the song and put on another. My Uncle had to cover his turntables because Steven was reaching for them to snatch the needle off. And here I am, along with my baby brother Stevie, trying to referee the battling DJs over what was an appropriate jam.

One of my beloved senior family friends gently guided me away from the action to the dance floor, so how could I refuse 83-year-old Mr. Orville? I stepped with him, but I watched. Steven was raving like a lunatic. It was just a record. My brother chilled out the entire situation. I have recently confirmed that Stevie told Steven if he didn't stop showing his behind at his sister's wedding that he'd have his whipped. I had five of my six brothers in the room, my surrogate brother in full Marine uniform – Master Sergeant Curtis Brookshire and my Daddy. It would not have been pretty.

Steven eventually made up with Uncle Johnny and they laughed about their "creative differences" and we jammed all night. His oldest sister danced so much her dress came undone. She actually pulled the boning out of it and was using it as a dance prop. We hollered! It was truly a beautiful way to begin a new life together. It seems like the wedding also restored the bitter relationship Steven had with his sisters. Weddings and funerals – they can bring a family together or tear you apart.

Since we were leaving so early the next morning for Hawaii, we had lots of business to handle before going to sleep. Our honeymoon suite became Business Office Central. Mommie Jo and Mama Mo helped us open all of our gifts, we had several thousand dollars in checks and cash. It took us hours to open them all, record them, endorse checks, complete deposit slips and pack. There were little piles at the front door to go to one person or another before leaving the hotel. By the time we showered and climbed into bed we were only going to have two hours of sleep. The consummation of this marriage was going to have to wait.

It took a complete 24 hours to get to Hawaii (remind me never to do *that* again), but the journey was well worth it. First stop on our 15-day honeymoon was the Mauna Kea Resort in Kona. Can you say mouth-hitting-the-floor luxurious?! Truly a paradise. Their beach was just lovely, and I had packed several books to read during beach and plane time. Steven was furious with me for reading books and reamed me up and down for bringing so many!

"You're not supposed to be reading books on your honeymoon!" he was downright angry.

"We're going to be here 15 days. I don't want to buy any books," I responded, my prudence preceding me.

By day two, I began getting a clicking in my jaw that made it difficult for me to open and close my mouth, which forced me to call the house doctor.

"Have you been under a lot of stress recently?" he asked.

"Well, I just got married and had a big wedding … " *And a new husband here acting like a jerk in paradise,* I said to myself.

"That'll do it. Relax. If you have never had this thing before, when your stress is minimized it will go away. It's called TMJ Disorder. Or lock jaw."

"I'll take that relax part under advisement!"

Steven and I were so exhausted all we did for the first three days was sleep and eat. We finally got around to consummating the marriage on day four. Rest was at the top of the list.

By day four, I began to wonder who it was I married. Steven visibly started acting differently. Making snide and rude comments about everything I had brought to wear, how I was combing my hair, what I was eating, my weight, and yes, my reading books.

I was hearing it from him, day and night. It got to the point where I would tell him I'd be right back and stay gone for an hour just so I wouldn't have to hear his mouth. We were at one restaurant in Maui and Steven was being so ridiculous to the waiter over an issue that he had no control over. I was totally embarrassed. I hid my face and tears streamed freely. The waiter kneeled down to comfort me, handed me a napkin and let me know very loudly he was unfazed by patrons like Steven.

He would always find something to perform over in a restaurant. I had told him, that with so many other people handling your food, this is not the place to pick a fight.

Him embarrassing me in public by treating someone rudely went on like that everyday. Steven was acting like a spoiled brat, a white aristocrat, who only knew how to operate from his place of entitlement. Then when he finished reaming Joe Public, he'd turn his venom on me. I cried my eyes out on my honeymoon every day, mainly because I knew I was sleeping with Dr. Jekyll or Mr. Hyde and I wasn't sure which. I'm not big on following zodiac signs, but he was a Pisces and this behavior was that up-stream, down-stream thing I'd heard people talk about dealing with in Pisces people. Testing the waters for the day to see which way the stream was flowing was apparent for his behavior. I'd have a lot to learn on the subject, obviously in Steven it was true.

Now I knew that there was a lot of stress leading up to the wedding, with finding an apartment, finalizing all of the plans, wrapping up at work, but hey… here we were in paradise, the drama was supposed to be over. Little did I know it was just about to unfold.

CHAPTER THREE

The Fire

"But his word was in mine heart as a burning fire shut up in my bones,
and I was weary with forbearing, and I could not stay."
Jeremiah 20:9

On December 18th, we finally arrived back in New York. Mama Mo met us at JFK Airport and drove us to Long Island for our car. I was so exhausted, but I wanted and needed to get to my own bed. I had to work the next day.

Steven had simmered down considerably. I knew the stress of it all had him acting cuckoo-for-cocoa-puffs! Mama Mo talked to him for hours about each detail of the trip. His talking to her seemed to take off his edge. I thought to myself, *so Mama Mo is the secret weapon to chilling him out. Got it!*

Back at work the word had already circulated in the industry about the loveliness of our wedding. There were so many people to talk to, but I had already been away from home and work for 20 days. Mental note: Never do *that* again.

At 2 a.m. on Friday, December 21st, we got a phone call from an operator asking for Steven to take a number and call his youngest sister.

"What has she gotten herself into now?" he questioned as he dialed the number.

When he spoke to her I only heard, "What's up…when?…how did that happen?…is?…" and then a scream that was stuck in his throat but the sound didn't come out of his open mouth.

I pried the phone away from his white knuckles. "What happened?" The news of what she said threw me back onto the bed.

There had been a fire at the house in Long Island. His sister had to jump out of the window on fire and was now at the hospital. Mama Mo was dead.

"Dead?" I repeated.

"Yes, dead. Y'all hurry up and get out here," she said calmly.

I picked up on her calm. "We're on the way." I thought, *Sweet Jesus!*

Steven had fallen onto the floor by the bathroom and was pounding it screaming, "Who am I going to tell all my secrets to now? Who am I going to talk to? My mother is dead! She was so good, she shouldn't be the one dead!"

I hugged him until his crying ceased. "Your sisters need you. I know things haven't always been great between you guys, but you need to stick together now more than ever, and they need you to be strong."

I said a quick prayer with him for our strength and while he washed, I laid out his clothes. We were out of the house in 15 minutes. From the car I called my parents, "We're on the way," said my Mommie.

Next call, Godmother Martha in California. Only a machine. Steven wanted me to leave the message. "NO way! Don't ever leave such a terrible message on someone's machine," I advised.

"Riiiight," he agreed.

The most bizarre thing happened while he was driving, he began executing road rage by trying to hit another car. He rolled down the window while driving and screamed at the dude in the other car, "Man, my mother just died, I ain't got nothing to lose. Just give me a reason!"

"Stop!" I screamed, "Stop the car right now!" He didn't listen. He kept gunning for the man with the car. Finally the guy turned off of the street and we drove top speed to Long Island.

The scene was like nothing you'd ever dream - firemen everywhere were still trying to put out the fire. There were also policemen and investigators, because there was a dead body in the house so it was officially a crime scene. The house was charred to a crisp. I threw up as soon as I got close. Steven's knees buckled as he ran toward the house calling his mother. Some of his neighbors helped him up and to a seat on the porch across the street. I had gotten a bad case of the shakes. My teeth were chattering and the tears kept pouring down my face.

Their neighbor, Mr. Ingraham recalled how he tried to save Mama Mo when the baby sister ran to his house with her three-year-old son. He said he got his ladder and put it up to Mo's bedroom window. He opened the window and he could hear her screaming. He told her to come closer to his voice, to climb out of the window, and that he was there to get her out. She kept screaming and he kept talking until the pressure from the fire blew out the window and it cut his head open. "I had to come down then," he conceded sadly pointing to his patched up head. I threw up again.

Day was just beginning to break and I remember thinking how beautifully orange the clouds in the sky were arranged as the sun promised its ascent. I was shivering so much, Mrs. Ingraham silently ushered me to her bedroom, flipped back her covers, took off my shoes, shoved me down and covered me up. I cried to myself just as God said to me, "Don't let me go." Two days back from the honeymoon, married only 20 days - - wow, it was clear to me that His hand was the only one worth holding.

After my nap, we arrived at the hospital to check on Steven's oldest sister. She had second and third-degree burns on her face, hands, arms and the back of her head. Fortunately for her, she fell asleep in a wool dress and a robe. As she was awakened by the screams of her mother, she jumped out of the window from the second floor of their split-level ranch home.

She was in need of skin grafting, hours of therapy, and had to be transported immediately to the burn unit at another hospital. Just as we were entering the hallway from the emergency room, the paramedics were rolling in Mama Mo in a black body bag.

Steven made the announcement, "They're bringing her in now." I threw up again and Steven shook his head and rushed to help me. A watchful nurse asked him how many times had I done such.

"Ever since she got to the house this morning," he answered, concerned.

The nurse took me into a room, rolled up my sleeve and pricked me with a needle. "You're dehydrated, Miss," she informed me as I looked up at the bag of saline drip. "Here drink this," as she handed me a bottle of orange-flavored Gatorade. I watched listlessly as the drip ran into my arm while Steven ran around the hospital checking on his sisters, collecting paper work and being a good big brother.

The hospital was packed with family and friends from the neighborhood when I finally got off of my drip. It was just what I needed. Now I could be of some help to everyone. We saw a cute, petite woman rushing toward us and Stacey's wife Claudette said, "Is that…Darlene?" The woman got closer. "Yep it sure is," she laughed nervously.

Darlene was Steven's ex-wife. I thought it was a friendly gesture for her to show up. Steven's eyes bucked out of his head. He hurriedly walked toward Darlene and turned her around in the other direction. They stood talking for a while and I saw him pointing to me. I heard her say she was really happy for him, but she was sorry about what happened and to advise her of the funeral's date.

His sister had such a long recovery time ahead of her, so it was decided that the funeral would be a memorial whenever she was able to attend a service.

My parents rolled into LaGuardia Airport that night as promised with helpful hands ready. My Mommie could see I had done a lot of crying and I didn't want to cry in front of her. Bo Daddy, Steven and other men searched through the house to see what they could salvage. They brought back garbage bags full of papers, clothes and photos.

Steven unzipped a black garment bag that had my wedding gown in it. That's right, Mama Mo brought it back with her from Chicago. The night we arrived from the honeymoon, she had asked me if I wanted to take the gown with me. Steven told her we'd be back over the weekend to get everything.

When I saw my gown all charred, I lost it. "Zip it up," I cried. "Just throw it out." I felt a terrible pit in my stomach that I couldn't quite explain.

Mommie was on paper duty, sorting and filing important papers that would be necessary for these children to piece together their past. It needed a meticulous eye and she was the right one for the job. She quietly called me over to read a yellow slip that was burned a bit in places, but still legible in others.

"Look at this," she eyed me as I read. My eyebrow went up at the hospital receipt for an HIV Antibody Test. It had Steven's name handwritten across the top. Mommie and I gave each other a quizzical look. She pushed and pointed me in Steven's direction and continued to look through the paperwork. With one eye up and both ears open, no doubt.

I cornered Steven in the music room, "Mommie found this," I said handing him the paper.

He barely looked at it, yet he knew exactly what it was. "Everybody's had a test at some point. It's nothing," he assured me and put the paper in his pocket with a kiss.

I sat back down and continued to go through the bags with Mommie. We didn't mention it again until he left.

"Well…" Mommie inquired.

"He said it's a test he took because everyone has taken one."

"Have you?"

"No."

"Me neither," she said flippantly.

"If we would have gotten married in New York, it's state law to take a blood test before marriage. But because we got married in Chicago, it was not a requirement."

"Humph, we'll see," Mommie said.

Meanwhile, the wedding video had arrived with a lackluster reception. None of us wanted to look at it with Mama Mo now dead. I watched it by myself first.

The videographer captured the wedding party for salutations. Steven's older sister said, "I want you all to have a good trip to Hawaii. Welcome to the family, LaJoyce. You just don't know, you're taking a lot off our hands, chile."

The younger sister said, "Congratulations you guys. LaJoyce, he's your problem now, don't send him back to our house!"

Mama Mo had wished us congratulations and ended her salutation with, "See Steven, I told you about all of that worrying. Everything always works out in the end," wink, wink.

I thought to myself, *what's that all about?*

I did notice how reverent Mama Mo was during Lencola's rendition of "The Lord's Prayer." Her hands were folded and she was totally prayerful and pensive.

I started to think about things she said that were beginning to make sense… *"Don't wait to get married," "I'm sending you to Hawaii because you'll never have this chance again,"* and her quiet praise during "The Lord's Prayer." Did she know something was going to happen to her?

When Steven's older sister did get out of the hospital a month later, we finally held Mama Mo's memorial service. Godmother Martha came from California and spoke at the service, where she admitted the two of them hadn't seen one another in 20 years before our wedding.

"We ran up and down the hall all night to each other's rooms giggling, and sharing secrets just like when we were young girls," she said from the pulpit. The church was packed and it was quite a somber occasion.

Steven and his sisters didn't have a lot of time to discuss plans for their future. During these conversations, it was like them against him. They had hateful, heated discussions with nasty flying words to each other. One thing was clear: There was no way - even with their mama dead and the home they grew up in burnt to a crisp - would the three of them ever again live under the same roof. When I suggested it, they all looked at me as if I'd lost my mind. Honestly, to marry amongst this mess, maybe I had. But it is said that death brings out the worst in people. And the three of them were a hot mess - - no pun intended.

I had to call my little brother Stevie in Chicago and make him vow that under NO circumstances would we act like that when the day comes to bury our Mommie. I made him promise that we'd make her proud even in her death. Because these children were acting like urchins who had never been raised right.

Mama Mo had worked nights as a nurse to get the high pay differential when her husband died years earlier. She saved and gave the three of them the best – maybe too much of it. Seeing them argue so viciously with one another made me sick.

"You all have too much business to sort out, and lots of decisions to make," I said, trying to referee. "You're going to have leave the past in the past to accomplish anything."

They were finally able to collect on Mama Mo's insurance policy, tear down the house and sell the land. This brought in a considerable amount of cash to be divided between the three of them.

Steven said he wanted to get out of New York state. I was all for that, because I had been five months away from going back to Chicago when we met. In my opinion New York had gotten all of the rent from me I intended to pay. In the eight years I lived in New York, I spent three-hundred-eighty-four-thousand dollars in rent!

There was no way I wanted to dish another dime and I didn't want to buy a house there because the taxes were just too ridiculous. That, in my mind, was too many new pairs of shoes.

So, with a new checking account full of cash, Steven's first stop was the travel agency. We sat there for many hours perusing brochures. I knew he wanted to go to the Caribbean so I focused on them.

"What's the name of that place in Jamaica you guys at work did a live broadcast from with Donnie Simpson?" he asked, totally interested.

"We've been to Jamaica 15 times, which place?"

"The one you said that was the ultimate in swanky."

"The Grand Lido? That place costs a fortune!" Always my prudence before me.

"That's the one!" He beamed, turned to the agent and announced, "The Grand Lido in Negril please."

She smiled and handed him the brochure.

When we left the travel agency, Steven had booked us first-class trips to Virginia Beach, Atlanta, Charlotte, Los Angeles, a Mexican Caribbean cruise to join my parents annual jaunt, and yes, Negril's Grand Lido. He wrote that woman a check for twenty-thousand dollars! I was absolutely flabbergasted.

"What's the occasion?" the agent wanted to know. Funny how when you spend a few dollars with people it gives them license to be all in your business.

Steven would tell anyone who would listen his story. "My mother just died and I deserve some happiness. My new wife and I are going to see the world."

He had lots of time at his job to take these trips. He told me I could take off without pay. The pay wasn't the point, who was going to write my programs? The career I had as a writer and producer wasn't just some job where my boss could call a temp agency and get a replacement, nor could they snatch a secretary to sit in my chair during my absence. So many days off meant putting a lot of strain on the other two writers and producers.

"Steven, I have to think about my job and this kind of money could be a down payment on our house."

"You're a wife now, not just some radio industry hustler. You don't even really have to work."

"Industry hustler!?..." I started to get pissed, but he shut me up with a kiss.

"I got it like that now. My mother wanted me to be happy with you. We're not going to get this opportunity again. Case closed."

I was pissed to the nth power, "Don't you ever call me an industry hustler again. I've worked my tail off in this business, I don't appreciate you minimizing my career."

One month later Steven got his wish. Sheridan Broadcasting Networks was moving its production unit to Pittsburgh. If I wanted to go there I could, but otherwise, I was laid off with one month's pay and the ability to collect unemployment. I was the first in my department to go and the others would follow in two months.

I had never seen my husband so happy that his wife didn't have a job. He was strange like that. Some things elated him, like this, and non-issue things sent him raging. He went out that night and bought me all sorts of things to setup my home office.

"You're going into business," he announced. "Look at how God worked out you being able to take all of our trips!"

"Yeah, look at that," I mused. I also noted that he conveniently thanked God when it suited him. Praised God when things were going his way. I'd been a reader of the Word for a long time and I knew that it was not my place to question Steven's salvation or the salvation he claimed to have. However, when you begin to come to church with me just to monitor the amount of money I'm putting in the collection plate, questions arise. I'm not exactly prying, but I'm definitely wondering.

For once we agreed the business would be great, especially since it didn't take all that much money to get me started with Retnuh Relations (Hunter = Retnuh my maiden name inverted). We specialized in publicity/production/programming. The production part meant radio, television and event production. With my additional phone line installed, I was officially in business with more clients than I could handle.

One of my largest clients was the New York Urban League. We were responsible for coordinating the entertainment aspects and all publicity for their annual Whitney Young Football Classic held at Giant's Stadium and all publicity. My team of four did an awesome job of generating hundreds of press hits and creating a tail-gate party with live entertainment from chart-topping artists. Superstars Will Downing and Eric Gable rendered "The Star Spangled Banner" and "Lift Every Voice And Sing."

I had been working day and night on this event, and on the big day I needed to be at the stadium very early. Steven decided for me that I didn't need to be there so early because in his mind I had done enough for the event but hadn't done enough while working on this project as a wife. He wanted us to hang pictures on the wall in our apartment. He then gathered the pictures he wanted hung, got the hammer and nails, and solicited my help.

"Steven, I need to be at the stadium in ninety minutes, are you taking me?" I asked calm as you please.

"Nope. Not until you take care of some of your wifely duties around here!" he ranted. "Are you helping me or not!?"

"Not today. I've got a show to do," calm still in check; sarcasm roaring. I called Mikey my teammate, play brother, and former Sheridan Broadcasting office-mate and producer to pick me up. Done. I washed my hair right quick, left Steven a ticket to enter the stadium, and went outside to sit on the stoop to wait for Mikey. Calm. I had a show to do.

Steven showed up at the stadium right at kick-off. I was soaring at the record-number attendance that we had helped to attain, and the first-ever tail gate party was a smash. I cuddled his arm and said, "Isn't this great!"

Prayer partner Lencola sat next to Steven and listened to him complain about my non-wifely actions of the day. She reminded him that he's the one who wanted me in business. "This is her business," she said waving her arms around pointing in every corner of the stadium. After this - - and because of the success today, there *will* be an after this - - it's on to the next event."

I thought, *Thank you prayer partner, well said. Amen.*

We spent most of 1991 taking the trips Steven had booked around the country, and we had a ball! We were in active pursuit of finding a new city to live. When we got to a Charlotte, Virginia Beach, and Atlanta, we'd be picked up by a realtor who would spend a couple of days showing us around their city. These places were very lovely, but none of them excited me enough to want to move there. Steven loved hot weather, and I loved cold weather and the drastic change in seasons.

Claudette and Stacey were taking a lot of quick trips to the Poconos in the mountains of Pennsylvania and invited us to their family home one weekend. They had a wonderful chalet at the end of a narrow, dirt road along a raging creek that Stacey's father had bought some 20 years before from a view in a helicopter.

Now, the Poconos were *beautiful* with lush vegetation you could smell, free-roaming deer, raccoons, beaver, bobcats, wild turkeys and bears. Steven was so relaxed in the Pocono atmosphere, he wanted to come back, so did I. Stacey agreed that anytime they came back we had a standing invitation to join them. Oh the times we had in that chalet!

On our rides up following Stacey on Friday nights, Steven and I created a song that started out as a whisper, "We're going to the Poconos." A little louder, "We're going to the Poconos." A little louder, "We're going to the Poconos." Screaming, "We're going to the Poconos!!!"

One three-day weekend up there with perfect weather to welcome us back, Steven was out exploring while Stacey and Claudette were having a major disagreement. As usual, I tried to referee, 'cause I could see this was about to spiral out of control. Just as I saw it spiraling, Stacey made the announcement, "Pack up everybody, I'm closing the house!"

I knew not to play with Stacey. I got up, packed our stuff and put it at the front door to wait for everyone else to get it moving. Steven came back hours later whistling and carrying a pizza. He almost tripped over the bags at the door, he looked at me and I shrugged.

In the car I said, "I don't want to go back to Brooklyn today."

"Me either. Let's just drive around and see what all is here." We got a motel room and set off on a mountain adventure by turning down roads we had never been on before that day. What we discovered were all of these communities tucked away where people lived full-time. Mmmmm, very interesting. The permanent resident homes were very different from the vacation houses.

Sunday afternoon a realtor was asking us what we wanted to see in property. I spoke up first. "Seclusion, acreage and water on the property," I said with a nod of approval from Steven.

"I've got just the place," she said. "It's a little ride so let's go."

The road up the mountain was so all the way up, that I was in the backseat getting car sick. There were so many turns, I was thinking, *This place is out' cause I can't make the ride.*

The property was on a dirt, dead end road, at the top of the mountain, but in a ridge with a stream winding through its three acres. I perched myself on a rock and looked around.

"This is it!" Steven exclaimed to me and the realtor.

"Yep, it is."

I asked, "How much?"

She looked at her papers, "Wow, this property is in foreclosure!"

I looked at Steven, we did our special move and slapped high five with our pointer's.

I sat right there on that rock praising God aloud because it seemed like we were right up there next to Him.

Within the hour, we had purchased that property and qualified for their payment plan, with the objective of building a house on it whenever we were ready.

We sang our little ditty the rest of the weekend changing *going* to *moving*, "We're moving to the Poconos…"

All of my projects had wound up for the year and I didn't want to just sit around from October until January with nothing to do. I went to work as a supervisor at TicketMaster. It was an easy, pay-every-week gig and just the thing I needed to keep me busy. I was devastated to find that I had to work on Christmas Day. Why in the world a ticket center was open on Christmas Day, I'll never know. Steven blew a head gasket going off about my hours.

We were supposed to enjoy the day in Queens at his cousin Charles' house. Charles was the patriarch of their family, and although he was a cousin, he was more like an uncle. I called him Uncle Charles then and still do today. Steven didn't feel that it was right for him to spend his first Christmas without his mother and without his wife, too.

I understood, but I was already committed until 5 p.m. I told him, "Go on to Queens and I'll meet you there." He didn't want to do it because he and his sisters still had mess brewing between them a year later.

I took all the money I had earned at TicketMaster and bought Steven an expensive piece of mixing equipment to aid in the production of the *Quiet Storm* Japan show he produced for WBLS air personality Vaughn Harper. And a blue-jean jacket airbrushed with my head-shot colorized on the back with "My Sunshine" scripted above it. Master artist Ricco, who did tour clothes for the stars, created it for him. The front had "Steve" scripted on one side and his Masonic emblem on the other. He didn't know when he was going off that I spent all of my money on him.

By the end of my shift at TicketMaster, the call volume was so low that they paid more for the staffing than they had earned for the day. I believe the main objective in my working there was to meet Ruth and her husband Clive, who was a computer repair man for Xerox.

Ruthie and Clive became like Claudette and Stacey to us. The three of us couples would have an incredible ball on a regular basis.

Ruthie and I both got fired from TicketMaster right when Retnuh Relations was gearing up again. My ego was a little bruised at getting fired from a twenty-thousand-dollar-a-year job that I only wanted to work for a short time anyway. The Holy Spirit reminded me that ego equals Easing God Out. Get over it. So I did.

Business was booming and Ruthie became my assistant. She had so many talents that were being wasted on the phones at TicketMaster I quickly discovered. I was a master organizer but Ruthie was the master blaster organizer! Her husband Clive, who we dubbed, "Mr. Computer Man," was a closet industry wanna-be producer. We all went to several record company parties and showcases together. He was so sweet that if I could help him get put on, great.

Clive had a computer purchasing program at his company through Macintosh and he got me my very first Macintosh so I could write all of the books I talked about and get them off of legal pads of paper and out of my journals.

Steven and Clive discovered they shared a love for guns and range shooting. Steven carried a gun with him all the time. He had many friends who were New York City policemen and he had a little shield from someone too.

Sometimes, Steven would act like he was a policeman if there was trouble in the street. I walked away from him trying to control a situation in our subway station one evening when we came home from a party. Maybe it was the alcohol he drank too much of. All I know is that my Steven was no policeman and had no business trying to control a potentially dangerous situation as if he were one. I literally ran home, because I couldn't stand to see the repercussions that may have arisen from his bravado. My Mommie always said, "When you see trouble, go the other way."

Steven and Clive went to buy shotguns and we took a long ride to the end of Long Island for a day trip to a shooting range in Montauk. They got Ruthie and I all setup with our ear mufflers and shooting target sheets 20 feet away. Ruthie barely hit the paper and we all cheered her on in fun.

I hit the target bulls-eye and Steven rejoiced, "Good Rabbit! I'm gonna move it back ten more feet. See if you can hit it, OK."

Bulls-eye. "You've got beginners luck today, honey."

"Something like that," I confessed.

Ten more feet back and bulls-eye. And again, and again. Finally at about 100 feet back, with a little crowd gathering, I slammed it again. Steven was visibly rattled.

Someone behind me asked, "What are you, some kind of marksman?"

I reloaded the rifle, "Uh, huh," and quickly changed the subject. "Here honey, it's your turn," handing everything over to him as if nothing had happened.

He stared at me sideways and sat down with a "why didn't you tell me" look. He didn't have a clue I had such skill. With a husband who made schizophrenic behavior a practice, being a sure-shot is a little something a girl may want to keep to herself.

My Grannie taught me how to shoot a gun out of the window into her backyard. Every time I went to her house, at night we'd shoot her 45 Smith & Wesson. She had a generous backyard in a noisy neighborhood where gunshots were not unfamiliar. She would say, "Hit this in the yard, hit that." During the day she would set up various objects and at night we'd shoot them out of the window. She taught me the fool-proof way how to shoot in marksman quality no matter how far away your target.

I'd go to a range with friends through the years and my love for rifles grew as did my skill. I've never been certified a marksman, but the marksman in me was evident just the same that day.

We moved to a large duplex apartment in a brownstone in Clinton Hills Brooklyn. It was absolutely awesome, with two bedrooms and three bathrooms, it better have been for sixteen-hundred dollars monthly not including utilities. All of our friends helped us do a one-day move. We provided pizza, pop, and junk food. It took us only about five hours to be totally moved in from six blocks away.

While we didn't have any children, we adopted my former student Karu. He stayed almost every weekend at our house even though he lived three subway stops away also in Brooklyn. The two of us got off to a rocky start when I was his Journalism teacher, but when I promised to call his mother - - and did - - about his classroom behavior, he did an about face.

Karu was a budding journalist and considered me his mentor, which was an honor because he had a special gift for writing and reporting entertainment news. He was a bright spot for me and Steven, and though he was a college-aged young man, Karu was wise beyond his years. We adored his company and for all Retnuh Relations projects, he was a great team member. He kept Steven rolling and his spirits high. It was a man thing. I knew Karu would grow up to become an awesome player in the entertainment industry and with his internet column "The Ru Report" of over 300,000 subscribers that he has recently retired, he did not disappoint me. Now days, he's not just my former student, but colleague, Pocono neighbor and friend.

I had begun a massive project with the National Black Leadership Commission on AIDS to coordinate their first ever Choose Life Benefit

Gospel Concert. I had to procure an all-star talent roster, gospel and secular, to perform for the benefit to be held at Abyssinnian Baptist Church. Additionally, there was a pre and post-reception, all to be put into motion by me. It was a huge undertaking, but I love huge projects. My team members were in place and we went to work.

The CEO and founder of the organization, Debra Fraser-Howze, is an incredible visionary, she could dream as big as I could execute. She and I were an unstoppable team. Debra became like a big sister to me. Our families are like family to one another even to this day, and it all came about from what she saw at the Urban League game the day Steven wanted pictures hung in our apartment.

With an awesome team in place, I felt comfortable enough to take the trip to out to California. First stop was to Godmother Martha's and then to my childhood buddy Dawn Keith, a then-budding comedienne and actress. Steven wasn't feeling well when we got to her house and she ordered him to lay down for a nap while we went for groceries.

"What's wrong with that baby?" Dawn quizzed me.

"I'm not sure, he came down with some bug and he's had the runs all morning."

"What's wrong with that baby?" she asked me again, stopping the car to look me in the face.

I looked at her strangely. Dawn was the drama queen of our bunch, but I didn't have a clue.

She exhaled deeply, "We've been friends since we were teenage girls and there ain't no secrets between us. I guess you'll tell me when you're ready."

I didn't know what Dawn was talking about, but for some reason T.D. Jakes was in the back of my mind preaching "Get Ready!, Get Ready!, Get Ready!"

CHAPTER FOUR

The Diagnosis

*"No weapon that is formed against thee shall prosper;
and every tongue that shall rise against thee in judgment, thou
shall condemn. This is the heritage of the servants of the Lord,
and their righteousness is of me, saith the Lord."*
Isaiah 54:17

By the time we arrived at our last stop of the Los Angeles tour, Steven was visibly sick and he refused to go to the doctor. He kept taking over-the-counter drugs to ease the symptoms that had overtaken him. The medicine he was taking did help some. He'd feel well enough to get dressed up and go to all of the activities we'd arranged, but by nightfall, he was sick again.

We had planned a dinner at legendary radio personality Frankie Crocker's home right before we left to get on the red-eye flight. Steven had taken really sick at a Sony Music party and we had to leave Los Angeles early. Frankie was really disappointed, because he liked Steven and was looking forward to hosting us at his home.

Frankie was like a father to me in the industry. I wrote scripts for him twice for events, and he bragged that I was the only person industry-wide who could put words in his mouth. That was the ultimate compliment from Frankie Crocker the Chief Rocker!

We had scheduled to take the red-eye because we both wanted to go to work directly from the airport. He called in sick and stayed in bed all day. I tried to get him to go to the doctor but he flatly refused. I whipped up a home-made soup and fresh bread for dinner. Soups and bread from scratch take forever to make with all of the chopping, dicing and kneading involved.

Steven woke up hungry and followed his nose to the kitchen. When I saw him I almost passed out. He was visibly blue!

I didn't want to alarm him. "How are you feeling?"

"Not that great but I'm hungry." I served him up some piping hot, chicken noodle vegetable soup.

"And when you finish that we're going to the emergency room. It's time you got some real medicine and found out what was wrong with you."

"I don't want to go tonight. I'll go in the morning."

I took his hands in mine so I could look at his fingertips. Blue. His oxygen wasn't circulating properly.

"My mother always said never go to an emergency room at night because the better doctors work days," he offered. "So I'll go in the morning and we'll drive out to Mercy Hospital in Long Island. I always promised my mother that if I got sick, I'd go to the hospital where she worked."

"We'll go wherever you want, just as long as you go," I said, wondering if he would make it through the night. Steven wanted to take a bath and we had a huge whirlpool tub for two. He hated baths and had never even been in it. I drew the water, but he said he was too weak to walk downstairs to get into it.

"Rabbit, draw me another bath up here."

He was beginning to scare me asking for things he'd never done before, first a bath and second to take one in the guest bathroom? He soaked in the tub for a couple of hours, letting out the cold water and running more hot. When he called me to help him out, his lips were blue and he was shaking even though the bathroom was a sauna.

"Are you sure you don't want to go to emergency now? We can go to Lenox Hill in the city."

"No!!!! I want to go to Mercy. I don't want to go to New York," he pleaded.

"OK, OK, OK," I conceded.

"Help me, I just want to lay down."

He refused the pajamas asking for a sweat suit instead. I got him dressed, laid him on the couch in the living room and covered him up.

Downstairs I called Godmother Martha, who is a nurse, about what was happening with him.

"Watch him through the night," she ordered. "Take him to the hospital first thing in the morning, don't delay."

I set the clock every hour and got up to check on him, because I was so jet-lagged from California I didn't trust myself to wake up.

By morning, Steven was listless, even more visibly blue, his lips were crusted over and his eyes were all glassy. He had no strength to even get to the car. I called our neighbor Dewanda for help to the car. She looked at me with a "what happened to him" stare. I shrugged, I didn't know.

In the emergency room, his vitals were all too low and they started plugging him up for monitoring, poking him to administer an

I.V. for his dehydration. He was going to be tested for every possible thing and that meant being admitted to the hospital.

A robust black doctor came in to introduce himself as Steven's doctor. We shot each other a "thank you Jesus" glance.

The doctor pulled up a chair to get eye-level with Steven laying down on the bed.

The doctor got right to it. "Have you ever been diagnosed with HIV?"

Steven's eyes got as big as a deer in headlights. "No, why would you say that?"

"Well, I'm not sure but all of your symptoms point to that or some kind of cancer?"

"Cancer?" we echoed like parakeets.

"I'm only speculating here, you guys, but all symptoms point to something very, very serious. You're going to be here a while until we find out exactly what that is."

On September 12, 1992, my husband of two years was now tucked away in a Long Island hospital for I don't know how many days until they uncovered the underlying cause of his symptoms. I had to switch gears back to business woman because I still had a show to do for an incredibly awesome cause.

I turned 30 on September 24th! My best-friend-in-the-whole-wide-world, Tyger, flew in just so we could go to an all-you-can-eat lobster feast. I took her with me to the hospital to visit Steven. Two weeks into his stay and they were still fuzzy on what exactly was wrong with him. He had a card and flowers for my birthday.

Relishing in their loveliness, I still tried to be prudent. "I hope you didn't buy these flowers in the lobby because they cost too much down there," I commented. Tyger pinched me in the back. "They're beautiful! Thank you honey!" I exclaimed in my do-over.

Steven handed Tyger an envelope. "Take my Rabbit out for a nice dinner since I can't, OK?"

"I promise," she said hugging him. "You get better fast, my best girlfriend needs you."

At dinner Tyger commented, "Steven looks bad, LaJoyce. What kind of hospital is this that they don't know what's wrong with him?"

"I know, and it's been two weeks already. He won't go to another hospital."

"Maybe he just wants to stay there in honor of his mother."

"I thought so, that's why I'm not pressing him. But they need to tell me something soon. Sleeping in a lounge chair and then driving to the city for work is really killing me."

"Don't say that girl, 'cause you ain't dead yet." She raised her glass, "Happy Birthday."

The very next day at the National Black Leadership Commission on AIDS office (BLCA), Steven's doctor called to say my husband was being relocated to the intensive care unit because he had a fever of 104 that wouldn't go down and that I should get there ASAP. I started crying.

"Doctor have you come up with a diagnosis yet?" I asked through tears.

"Well, there are still several more tests to be done like ...." And he named everything under the sun except what I was listening for.

I interrupted him, "Have you tested him for AIDS?"

"Well, you can't just test people for AIDS. I mean you need consent and then there is a whole counseling component and..."

I interrupted him with a fit of screams and tears but very focused. "You have had my husband in the hospital for two weeks and have no clue what is wrong with him! If there is a possibility he may have AIDS then you could have tested him and counseled him by now!"

Debra appeared in the doorway listening to the ruckus, feeding me tissues and agreeing with me. That doctor didn't know that I was sitting at THE premiere Black agency for policy on AIDS in the nation. He didn't want me to put him on the phone with Debra, who was just waiting for the opportunity to pounce on him, with her member of the Presidential Advisory Council on AIDS title. I wanted the doctor chewed up, but not like Debra would have given it to him.

"Test my husband for AIDS today and don't let me ask you again!" I ordered. Debra offered great comfort but sent me on my way, and I jumped the subway to Brooklyn to my car.

While I was driving the Holy Spirit said to me, *"open your hands."* I looked at the brewing traffic jam, balanced my palms on the wheel and stretched open my fingers. I felt an incredibly warm sensation going through them, and I praised God right there for the anointing that He was giving me. When I got to the hospital, I knew exactly what to do.

Steven was in ICU drinking chocolate milk. "Rabbit, you're not supposed to be here today. Don't make Debra mad," he teased. If he only knew what happened earlier. I kissed his head but I didn't say anything. I was speaking in the Spirit under my breath as I flipped back the covers. I rubbed his feet, legs, thighs, belly, arms and up to his ears.

"That was a drive-by massage. You'll be better soon. I love you," I said and I kissed his forehead. I told the nurse on the way out, to contact me at work when his fever went down and left her the number. We had an all-nighter to pull for the event. I bounced out of the building singing a song of praise. Two hours later at the office the hospital called to say, Steven was back in his room and that his temperature was stabilized. Hallelujah!

The First Annual Choose Life Benefit Gospel Concert went off without a hitch on October 12, 1992, at the Abyssinian Baptist Church in Harlem. The line-up included Donnie McClurkin, Ashford & Simpson, Tramaine Hawkins, Donald Malloy and Elder Timothy Wright & Choir. The host was Clifton Davis and the sermon was delivered by the Reverend Jesse Jackson.

Tyger and her brother Ronnie flew in special to be with me for this black-tie affair, which turned out to be an absolute sold-out success. Donald Malloy brought the house down and thinking about Steven, I excused myself from the sancuatary and ran to the stairwell to cry. Donald had ushered a new realm of the Holy Spirit that grabbed hold of me and wouldn't let go.

Bishop Sam Williams, with whom I co-hosted a gospel radio show for several years, and Tyger saw me run out and they both came to comfort me. Only the presence of the Holy Spirit was comforting me at that moment, and my anointed and appointed friends there encircling me.

Godmother Martha flew in to see about the situation first hand. My telephone reports were no longer satisfactory. Being a nurse, she came in and completely took over our the hospital and my kitchen. I was barely eating and she made me the best food ever. We had a different steamed fish every night. She made me come home for dinner instead of camping out at the hospital.

I had seen Steven get pricked, poked and prodded in every direction. When they tapped in to his spinal column to drain fluid, and took a piece of bone out of his spine, my goose was cooked. I didn't need to see all of that. Bearing witness to the awesome healing machine God made of the body convinced me to continue to take better care of myself.

Debra summoned me into a behind-closed-doors conversation in the conference room at BLCA. The next day, the family was going to an emergency meeting called by the doctor at the hospital. After 40 days, it was confirmed that Steven in fact had pneumonia.

"Have the doctors mentioned the term PCP to you?" Debra asked concerned.

"No, because I don't know what that is."

"It stands for Pneumoncystis carinii pneumonia. It is in association with people who are HIV positive. I need you to brace yourself for what the doctors will tell you tomorrow. And I need you to call me the minute after you meet with them."

Brace myself? The scripture from Psalms 18 showed up in my face plain as day, *"He is a buckler to all those who trust in Him."* I could only brace myself if I had something to hold onto. Jesus had been my rock thus far, and he'd be my brace now.

The meeting invitees to the hospital were Godmother Martha, Uncle Charles, and me. The doctor called me into Steven's room alone and sat down. I sat on the edge of the bed and held Steven's hand.

"Rabbit, I just want to let you know that your husband has AIDS."

Jesus was holding me up - - braced. I hugged him tightly, but I didn't cry. I looked over at the doctor for answers only he could provide.

"Steven is not just HIV positive, he has full-blown AIDS. Currently he has a T-Cell count of four. A healthy person has a T-Cell count of 1200 to 1500. When he walked into the emergency room, Steven was on his way out. At this point we need to get him on a round of anti-viral medications and then find him an infectious disease doctor. Do you understand all of this?" he asked.

"Yes, I do." I didn't feel the need to go into where I had been doing a project for the last three months. He was a doctor, it was his duty to explain. After taking 40 days to tell me what was wrong with my husband, the least he could do was explain. I wasn't angry. I didn't ask where he got it. After working at BLCA I had come to learn that once a person was infected, that was all that mattered - - do something about it from there.

Braced, I asked, "What else?"

"There is a nurse who is also an AIDS counselor for the two of you outside. She will let you know how you will get tested and what you can do to protect yourself."

I'm thinking, *how am I going to protect myself with my husband?* Yeah, send her on in here.

Stevie asked me to stay while he told Uncle Charles and Godmother Martha together. Tears immediately popped into Uncle Charles' eyes and he wiped them really hard and shook his head as if someone hit him in the head with a bat.

Godmother Martha jumped into nurse mode, quizzing the doctor, "How long do you think he has before he becomes full-blown?"

"He's full-blown now, his T-Cell count is four," answered the doctor. The news of his status rocked her further.

This little meeting was so carefully orchestrated that I bet the doctor and Steven rehearsed every line. It sounded and felt that way to me.

Uncle Charles and Godmother excused themselves while the nurse came in to speak with us.

"I have to offer you counseling sessions before you can take the HIV test. This is a Catholic hospital and it is just procedure."

"Miss, you can take my blood right now," I said rolling up my sleeve. "I don't need any counseling, I've already counseled with the Master Doctor." Like Bishop Sam says - - The Consultant, whom the consultants consult!

Steven piped up, "My wife is very religious."

"I'm not religious, I have a personal relationship with Jesus."

"But the counseling is a preparation for what is about to happen now and after," said the nurse convincingly.

"Rabbit, I think you should get the counseling just in case," Steven said sympathetically.

God walked into the room and sat next to me on the bed. I felt a boldness in Him that was unstoppable. "Take my blood now so you can tell me I'm negative! Since this is a Catholic hospital, I'm sure you believe in Jesus and the power of His blood, or do you. I'm covered in it and I'm whole."

"Well, I have to advise my supervisor that you are denying counseling. And then I'll call you with a date to come in to do it."

"Don't wait 40 days like you did to tell me about Steve," I said over-politely. "I deserve the right to take that test ASAP. And if I can't do it here quickly, I'll go somewhere else."

She was so flustered with me! When we all simmered down over the testing issue, she shared some very valuable tips on how to maneuver with a mate with AIDS.

"Are you all having protected sex?" she asked.

"Sometimes yes, sometimes no," Steve answered.

"How often do you have sex?"

"Often", we both answered.

"It is now important to always have protected sex," she urged.

I thought, *Well, I hope Steven's had enough sex to last him cause I'm done.* A rubber is a device that is not 100 percent effective. If it can't protect you from pregnancy, how can it protect you against AIDS? It's a rubber, and the last time I checked, rubbers leaked.

If this was the type of counseling service the nurse was offering to couples, it was failing miserably. How in the world do you even fix your face to tell a woman to have protected sex with her husband? Who, by the way has AIDS. Absolutely ludicrous.

"Bleach kills the virus, so always use it when cleaning the bathroom, in the wash and on dishes." Steve and I threw each other a knowing look. At the time, I was the bleach-everything-in-the-house queen. If I had to be stuck on a desert island with only one cleaning product, back in those days it would have been bleach.

Miss Nurse promised she'd call me in a week to schedule the test that she would administer herself. "If you change your mind about counseling..."

I cut her off, "I need you to respect my position of faith on this one. I'm walking through this fiery trial and through the valley of the shadow of death. I fear no evils, not even AIDS."

She sealed her departure with a hug. She was clear.

Debra picked me up the next day in Brooklyn and drove me to the Gay Men's Health Crisis. They were closed, as it was a Saturday, "Whaaat, they should never be closed!" she said furiously. "First thing Monday morning you make an appointment with their intake department so you guys can receive the goods and services for P.W.A's - - people with AIDS," she ordered.

Steven wanted me to have his sisters at the hospital on Sunday so he could tell them all one by one. I spent the night at Stacey and Claudette's to tell them as he had requested and to be near the hospital. I was so wound up, I couldn't sleep. I lounged on the couch in their living room and watched TV all night. Stacey got up every other hour to turn off the TV and I'd wave at him to show I wasn't sleeping.

By 7 a.m., I heard him and Claudette discussing my sleepless night because they have lots of photos of me sleeping soundly at parties. If I stayed awake for any reason all night, there must be a big problem. I knocked on their door and sat on the edge of their bed.

"I haven't been able to sleep because Steven wanted me to talk to you both but I didn't know how. We had a meeting with the doctor and Steven has AIDS."

Stacey grabbed his face and burst into tears. I got off of the bed and held him until he stopped crying. Claudette sat helpless watching her husband. There was nothing she could do for him. Steven and Stacey had been best friends since they were young kids. When we got to the hospital, Stacey ran into the room and hugged Steven with all of his might. I'm glad he didn't do any more crying, at least not in front of him.

Steven wanted Claudette and Stacey to stay in the room while he told his baby sister first, but Stacey excused himself and I knew why. When he told his baby sister, she fell into a fit of tears. When the two of them were together, they were very civil to one another until the older sister arrived on the scene. They'd definitely be girls against boy.

The older sister sat in the chair with her legs crossed swinging her foot. When he told her, not even breaking a swing with her foot she said, "I knew that."

Steven asked, "What do you mean you knew that?"

"Mama knew it and she told me," she said. I felt like the tennis ball being belted from one side of the net to the other following this conversation.

My mind flashed back to the wedding video, *"LaJoyce, you're taking a lot off our hands chile."* *"He's your problem now, don't send him back to our house."* *"See, I told you about all that worrying, everything always works out in the end – wink, wink."* Nahhh, and I shook it off.

"Shut up, you're lying, shut up! I hate you!" he screamed at her. Then he went off with his brother-versus-sister tirade, "Every since we were little…" I couldn't believe that he was taking it there, in the middle of his death announcement from a hospital bed.

"I hated you then and I hate you now! Get out of my room!"

She got up calmly and walked out. Claudette and I stared at each other like "did-that-just-happen?"

The day of the fire, God said, *"Hold on to me and don't let go."* That kept flashing through my head like a blinking yellow light.

Now that the immediate family and close friends were informed, the sisters called a meeting to discuss how we would handle this news with the public-at-large. It was the youngest sister who took charge, "We are going to tell everybody that Steven has stomach cancer."

"Why stomach cancer?" I asked.

"Because since he had been in the hospital a lot before for ulcers, then it seems normal that he might get stomach cancer," she reasoned.

"Really," I said, unconvinced.

"All right everyone, are we clear? Steven has stomach cancer."

I had wished that the declaration of stomach cancer were true, then there would have been no cause for concern of my health. That little issue neither of them ever seemed to mention. I didn't care if I ever took the test. I knew I was negative, and in that knowing, I had peace.

See, I didn't just start praying when this showed up in my life. I had been God's girl for a long time. This was a test to see how I could stand in what I'd learned about prayer – then I relaxed in my faith. I know God and He definitely knows me. I love how I discover something new about Him each day. One of my favorite songs from Saint John that we used to sing was… *"Morning by morning new mercies I see. All I have needed thy hand has provided. Great is thy faithfulness, Lord unto me."*

It was another full week before Steven was released from the hospital. He had withered down to skin and bones. His six-foot-three frame was all of 125 pounds. My job was to bring him home and go to work rebuilding him in his own bed and with food from my kitchen.

The first stop he wanted to make was to the office of the attorney we dealt with after the fire. He handled all the legal aspects of Mama Mo's estate. The attorney looked at Steven barely filling up a sweat suit. It took him every ounce of energy he had to walk from the car to the office. He was so totally winded and exhausted by the time he got to the couch that when I sat him down, Steven toppled over. I sat down next to him and laid his head in my lap while I delivered the news.

The attorney stopped flipping his pen. "I'm so sorry Steven. How can I help you?"

"I want you to make out my will and leave everything to my wife here. I don't want my sisters to get nothing I have," he spat with venom. "One of them killed my mother by leaving that candle burning and they won't say who did it. I hate them for killing my mother!"

"All right," the attorney said, looking at me. He was all too familiar with the family feud between that bunch.

At one point right after the fire, Steven wanted to sue his sisters for reckless endangerment, or attempted homicide. It was eating him up and he would not let it go. He even went so far as to ask other people what they thought about the idea. Fortunately they all thought as I did, that it wasn't a good thing to pursue. The problems those siblings had to work out happened long before their house burned down, before their mother died in it, and before Steven got AIDS. However, this latest development in their lives was just another log on the fire to compound their complex relationship.

Steven asked, "How long will it take for you to make out my will? Because I don't know how much longer I have."

"Right away, I can have it in two days," assured the attorney.

It was a laborious process for us to get in the car. Steven may have weighed only 125 pounds, but it was all dead weight. He had zero strength. He laid the car seat to the reclining position and fell into a deep sleep as if he'd been working on the railroad all day. Fortunately for him, I had to do the pharmacy and grocery store run so he got to sleep for more than two hours before getting home. He needed every minute of it to regain his strength to get from the car to the bed. Again, another deep sleep for two hours.

Dewanda came over and helped me organize myself. She and her roommate Lucy loved them some Steve. During the year we had lived in that brownstone we had lots of activity in our backyard, which was separated from Dewanda's and Lucy's by a fence. We used to pass Dewanda's 2-year-old daughter over the fence so she could hang out with us, as well as the sharing of many meals.

Lucy kept Steve company while I made dinner. I was grateful to for their strong, supportive and silent company. I didn't have to keep discussing the dilemma over and over with them. They were among the first set of people to whom I divulged the family secret. They were a part of the village I had created for myself since my family was not in New York. One of the first things I was able to accomplish was the assemblage of a group of people that I call family.

His sisters knew he was getting out of the hospital, where were they on that Friday he came home? Where were they for the rest of the weekend? It was our friends who came to visit, help around the house and bring well wishes. Karu practically moved in and he was a beacon of light for us both. We didn't see his sisters at our house for a week, and Steven talked about how it made him sad every day.

I had accepted a full-time position at BLCA as the Director of Communications and my start date was the same day I had to take the AIDS test. I got to the hospital early and waited for the nurse outside of her office.

"You're awfully dressed up this morning," she acknowledged.

"I start a new job today at the Black Leadership Commission on AIDS in the city."

She looked at me, "Really?"

"See how God placed me right when I needed to be there?" The look on her face told me she didn't understand.

"This organization has been around for ten years and I'd never heard of it until a month before Steven came to the hospital. Their office is headquarters for all of the information and resources a person could want about AIDS for people of color in New York City, and here I was working there at the time of his diagnosis."

"Yes, I see," she said finally beginning to understand.

I sealed it for her further, "Nobody but Jesus could have executed that plan any better. Just like He's kept me covered in the Blood even though I was having a whole lot of contact with a person with AIDS."

"You sure have a lot of faith," she said.

I rolled up my sleeve and gave her my arm, "Yes, I do. So please hurry and take my blood, I have to get to work."

The director of the BLCA office, Bill, didn't know I had to take my test that morning, so he had called my house looking for me. He said at first he panicked because he thought I had changed my mind. My BLCA family also knew about Steve because they knew AIDS intimately. It was their work and I was not in the mood for hiding this bit of information from the very people who could help us.

Debra had a serious talk with me about personal stuff. "Are you and Stevie kissing?"

"Not now, cause he's got thrush in his mouth," I told her.

"Make sure you kiss a while after he's brushed his teeth. Sometimes a person's gums bleed when brushing. So, if infected and you kiss, that can be a point of transmission."

"I haven't read that one."

"You won't. They can't release that information to the community without really knowing all the details, and doing several double-blind studies and all. But it's a body fluid ain't it?"

"You're right. Then what about sweat?"

She just pointed to me, like, yep.

"And tears?"

She raised an eyebrow. I exhaled through my teeth.

This thing was no joke! But these details, while not "written" anywhere, any critical thinker could figure this one out. I received all that on the first day at my new job. Thank you Lord.

I purposely waited until I took the test to tell my parents about Steve because I didn't want them worried about my status for too long. But mainly because they were a loving, but seriously crazy bunch. Sure enough, when I gave them the news, they flipped.

Mommie gasped, "What are you going to do?"

"I'm going to stay here and take care of him."

"I'm coming to get you," Bo Daddy said.

I pleaded, "Come on y'all, I need you to stick by me and understand my decision. I need y'all to exhibit some of that compassion you taught me to have."

Bo Daddy flipped, "All I'm saying is, you didn't sign up for this. You know you don't have to stay. Pack up."

"Mommie please, don't let him come here."

"Honey, hang-up the phone!" He hung up muttering.

She was calmer now, "What about you? Oh, Lord. Are you OK?"

"I took my test this morning, I'll have the results in a couple of weeks. And yes, I'm OK and I'm negative."

"How do you know?" she asked.

"God told me so, and I'm standing on the Word you taught me," I reminded her.

"I know, I know. But listen, remember that burned yellow slip of paper we found after the fire that had Steven's name on it from an HIV test that he said was nothing? I told you we'll see," she said reminding me.

Through all of this, I had totally forgotten about that. It was two years ago. That's what Mommies are for, to remind you of life's little things that one day will mean something big.

"I remember now. I need you to call a family meeting to tell them. His sisters want us to tell everyone that he has stomach cancer. I will tell people that lie who are not a part of our lives because he does deserve to have his privacy protected, but some people have just got to know."

"I think I should wait until you have your test results before I tell everyone else."

"Good idea."

"Do you need me to come?"

Not now," I said exhaling, "but I will. Mommie, you brought me to Jesus. Remember, He'll never leave us or forsake us. I'm negative, you'll see."

My friend Patti, whose parents are preachers, assembled a group of my mighty prayer warriors for a conference call with people from all over the country who knew of Steven's situation. It included Mommie, Lencola, Tyger, Henzy, Bishop Sam, Patti's parents, friends from LA, and Atlanta. The objective was to lift up a prayer corporately to expedite his healing. There must have been 20 people on the call. Everyone took turns praying, worshipping, speaking in tongues. It was totally awesome. I was overcome with the Spirit and at the words lifted to God on our behalf. Patti was staying the night at our house. I heard her hang up the extension and run to my room when I started to cry. She was a P.K. so she knew how to pray, lay hands and seek the Lord's face.

During the wait for the results, Steven was a new man. He had changed his talk, and judging by the Bible laying next to his night stand he was trying to change his walk too.

"I'm so glad we're moving away, I can't wait to get out of here. Maybe we should go ahead and build that house in the Poconos right now. That way when we get sick, we'll be away from here together…"

"Wait! Wait! Wait! Whatever do you mean when *we* get sick?

"Rabbit, you may not want to deal with the fact that you may be positive, but I have been thinking a lot about it."

"Don't waste your time. Don't claim something for me that isn't so!" I fumed.

"All I'm saying is that one of us needs to look at reality."

"My reality is that God has kept me covered and will continue to cover me. End of story."

Steven had conjured up these convoluted visions of us getting sick together, and then dashing off to some other place to live so we could die. Now that was a web of deception he was spinning in his own mind.

Two weeks later, the nurse called me to her office for the results. I was annoyed at how she was delaying telling me I was negative, but I let her have her moment.

"Your results came back negative," she beamed.

"Thank you Jesus!" I praised.

"I have learned to have more faith because of you," she testified. "We all actually thought there would be two cases of AIDS here, but you were so sure you were negative. I've been a nervous wreck waiting for these results to come back and you didn't even seem worried."

"No I wasn't worried because if you're going to pray, why worry, if you're going to worry, why pray. There really was no need to waste one night's sleep over it. Well, I did lose one night's sleep when I had to tell Steven's best friend, but that's it."

I could tell that this woman was religious. She had all of the artifacts a lot of Catholics have around that let you know they're Catholic. This nurse was a woman of faith, but she failed to bring her faith to work. She hadn't yet activated her faith into full operation, because if she had, she'd never be able to separate it from her. Also, she wouldn't have been so surprised to see faith at work in someone who knew how to activate it. I understood very clearly, that it was my faith that had made me whole.

God's hand was holding me through this test. I've learned to discern the hand of God by coming out of what could have destroyed me.

CHAPTER FIVE
The Care Giving

"But be ye doers of the word, and not hearers only,
deceiving your own selves.
For if any be a hearer of the word, and not a doer, he is like unto
a man beholding his natural face in a glass: For he beholds
himself, and goes his way, and straightway forgets what manner
of a man he was.
But whoso looks into the perfect law of liberty, and continues
therein,
he being not a forgetful hearer, but a doer of the work,
this man will be blessed in his deed.
James 1:22-25

From the moment I told Steven I was negative, he went back to his Jekyll and Hyde routine. At first I could not understand why he was so ornery. I made sure that I did not flaunt my negative status around him, but as my peace increased, his meanness increased. Ruthie was Steven's full-time care giver during the day while I worked at BLCA. She had been a nurse's aid at one time and she knew all about taking care of sick people. Retnuh Relations needed to add another department, the Florence Nightingale division.

As directed by Debra, we went to the Gay Men's Health Crisis (GMHC) for our intake appointment so Steven could be registered for goods and services. They had a flight of stairs to the counselor's office and after Steven made them, he had to lay down, as always with his head in my lap. He was so exhausted he could barely answer the questions.

"How do you think you contracted the virus?" asked the counselor.

"I don't even know. I'm not sure," he answered shakily.

"Steven was married before and his wife was a drug abuser who had relations with other men," I offered. Steven had never even considered that until I said it.

The counselor reluctantly agreed, "That's a real possibility." The statement was not finite, it had a hint of "but-what-else-is-there?" waving in the air from him.

"Is your ex-wife infected?" the counselor logically asked.

Steven seemed wary of the line of questioning, "I haven't spoken to her so I honestly don't know."

GMHC loaded us down with information, Ensure drinks to help boost his weight and loads of rubbers. There was an appointment made for a nutritionist to come to our apartment so that he could get on the road to gaining weight and strength back.

I began making the Ensure drinks in various ways so that he could get them down without being bored. I'd make the chocolate and strawberry flavors with crushed ice like a milkshake. I'd heat the chocolate flavor and serve it like hot chocolate and the vanilla, I would freeze really cold and serve it with breakfast like milk.

I knew that the AIDS medication was to increase his viral load, but it was destroying everything else in its path. I made teas with immune building properties like dandelion, red clover, alfalfa, goldenseal, and Echinacea. He hated drinking it but I'd stand over him with an Ensure treat to drink right behind it. Twice a day I'd also make him a smoothie with spirulina, chlorophyll, blue-green algae, barley, wheat grass and flax seeds. I'd blend it with frozen fruits like strawberries, apples and bananas in fruit juices.

It was mandatory that he drink a cup of aloe vera water every hour he was awake. The water was to keep his elimination tract open and to run the toxins from the medication out of his body. I made the aloe water by freezing the plant and then cutting the frozen pieces and placing them in water containers like ice cubes. He complained that it was bitter and it had him running to the bathroom too much.

"When you get to the point where you can literally run to the bathroom, you can stop drinking so much." My methodology was also in an effort to get him out of that bed, from in front of the television for some exercise. Any person who laid in the bed for 40 plus days, hooked up to a catheter, seriously needed exercise.

Every other day, I'd dry brush his entire body and put him in the Jacuzzi tub for a Dead Sea salt soak. The dry brushing helped to slough off the dead skin and to stimulate the circulation, and the Dead Sea salts draw toxins from the body that were ready to be eliminated but needed a little help.

His face had broken out terribly, a reaction from all of those medications in his system undoubtedly. So every night I gave him an egg white facial since his skin was oily. He'd relax with the facial on while sipping his green smoothie through a straw. When the egg mask had hardened, I used warm towels to melt the mask and then wipe it off. He loved this ritual and his face started to clear.

I created meals high in carbohydrates and protein. Every meat dish had mashed potatoes with gravy, or a baked potato with real butter or brown or basmati rice with gravy. We always had my garbage salad first and it could have been a meal all by itself, and at least one fresh cooked vegetable like green beans, collard or turnip greens, beets, turnips or cabbage.

I had a bread maker and it seemed to never stop churning out loaves. Every meal, three times a day he was served with a chunk of homemade bread toasted warm, with butter. Depending on the meal, I'd whip up some sweet cornbread or hot water cornbread for a diversion. Once weekly, we had a pot of lima beans, great northern beans, lentils, or red beans and brown rice as the main event. Steven was in hog heaven. Like my Grannie would say, "make sure you keep pot on your stove."

"Rabbit, these meals are so good, but can a brother get a pork chop?" he would ask knowing the answer already.

"Absolutely not! No pork chops, no pork bacon, no pigs feet, no ox tails!" I admonished. "I'll make you a deal, when you feel well enough to drive yourself to the store, and buy the pork chops yourself, I'll fry them up real crispy just the way you like them."

"Deal!" he said with a mouth full of bread.

At his next doctor's visit he had gained a full ten pounds in the fifteen days he'd been out of the hospital! The doctor was amazed with his at-home recovery. When he asked me what I was doing, he couldn't wrap his head around it all. He didn't at all agree with the herbal stuff, but he admitted he didn't fully understand it either.

Steven got a little peeved, "With all due respect doctor, I was in the hospital here all of these weeks and I kept feeling worse and worse. The food sucks, the beds are hard and you're pumping me with all this medicine. Whatever the wife is doing for me, I'm going to keep doing it because I really feel better. Not great, but better."

I thought, well, well, well. Since our health regimen proved to show steady improvements we faithfully kept it going.

By Christmas, he was able to walk around the house and go up and down the stairs in our duplex with little effort. My parents came for Christmas and I had bought them Broadway show tickets.

Steven had chosen to taken up the art of selective prudence. He argued with me about the present of the ticket purchase in front of my parents. He also got in my face and ordered me not to move the car to drive them to the theater, which was appropriately parked for alternate-side-of-the-street parking the next day. He was so busy in my face arguing and fussing on the narrow staircase, that he fell backwards down the steps for no apparent reason.

"I keep telling you to quit fooling with me, I'm God's girl for real," I chastised. "You'll figure it out."

I marched out of the house with my parents in tow, got in the car and drove them to the city. My parents were fuming.

"That boy done gone stark, raving mad!" Bo Daddy assessed. "You need to get away from that fool."

Mommie sucked her teeth, "Huh, I don't know how you deal with him, myself. He's always huffing and barking at you. I don't care what's wrong with him, he has no business trying to get all in your face like that, LaJoyce."

This was the worst possible thing for my parents to see. It was also the worst thing for Steven to pull for the first time. This wasn't his family he was trying to get bad in front of, it was mine. Did he actually think that my parents were going to co-sign his anger over moving the car!

Parking places in our neighborhood were tight, but I found that if you said a little prayer right before turning the corner, there would be one waiting for you or someone would pull out just in time. He called me nutty to think that way, but it always worked while I was driving. Now that he was sick, he got to see it work more and more.

We started off the new year right with Bishop Sam hosting Bible study at our house. We had regular attendees in Lencola, Arlene (my girl from college), my client Pepsi, Clive and Ruthie. We had a love seat, and the left corner was designated the "crying corner." It never failed, because whoever sat in that corner had some kind of break-through or a tearful testimony every week. Bishop Sam always had incredible lessons and Steven respected him the most over any other man of the cloth.

By February 1993, Steven had gained his weight back and was working again. To look at him, you would have never thought he had full- blown AIDS. The doctors were all confounded at his miraculous recovery. They had not told us, but they didn't think he would live two weeks after leaving the hospital.

I was so burnt out from taking care of Steven that I resigned from my post as Director of Communications at BLCA. It was just too much for me to do AIDS at home and at work. The emotional strain was starting to tax me. I knew I had to bail out before I suffered a nervous break down. I wasn't frail to the point of having one, but I felt it coming if I didn't make some changes.

My client roster with Retnuh Relations was in full-swing with clients like author of the self-published book *Invisible Life*, E. Lynn Harris, *Billboard* Magazine's Pre-Grammy Party and Dreamologist Dr. Pepsi.

I had to coordinate the *Billboard* Magazine Pre-Grammy Party for the industry-ites. The manager of the *Billboard* R&B Chart, Terri Rossi, was an industry luminary and my mentor. We landed a major coup by garnering the attendance of Aretha Franklin and James Brown. The attendees list was the who's who of the business as well as the artists to be awarded.

The party was a formal affair so Steven and I wore matching Franklin Rowe outfits. The party was for one thousand very VIPs and security had to be tight.For the first time, I had the need to get Steven involved in an event. Since he liked playing police, I put him in charge of security. He called his group the Lakeview Connection because he went back to his Long Island neighborhood and got 20 from his crew to stand watch. On that night he was the party police. Steven, Stacey, Claudette and the others were a superb crew and Steven had coordinated it all.

In other business, E. Lynn Harris was a friend of mine since the early 1980s. He, like Lencola, is from Arkansas. Lynn always said he dreamed of a career as an author and I volunteered to help him when he self-published a novel called *Invisible Life*.

Steven could not stand Lynn. I mean down-right hated him. Every time I mentioned his name, Steven would say, "Don't mention that faggot's name in front of me." If Lynn would call he'd say, "Tell that faggot not to call here when I'm home," loud enough for Lynn to hear. "How can you call yourself a Christian and have gay friends!" I thought, No he didn't have the nerve to go there.

Steven totally embarrassed me when he cussed Lynn out on the phone for utilizing our FedEx number, which I said he could use. Steve demanded he send the money ASAP and told him to never use our account again. Lynn was just getting started back then, so hey, if I could share my FedEx number with him to send a few books around, why not?

I had enough of Steve. "You may not like my gay friends, but they were here for me in this city long before you came along. Lynn and I have been through more together than you and I will get to go through for a life-time. We're friends forever! Get over it!" I never mentioned him again to Steve. To this day, Lynn and I are still friends.

We started taking weekend trips to the Poconos again, in search of the right builder for our home. We had met a wonderful sister in our new community named Ellen who opened her home to us on weekends until we were situated. Once we decided on a builder, we found a house to rent nearby until ours was ready, for only 700 dollars! That was going to be a huge savings for us. Claudette and Stacey also planned to make the move to the chalet and we decided we'd all do it together.

A couple of weeks before we were to move, Steven was shopping his brains out. He went to Saks Fifth Avenue and purchased an eleven-hundred-dollar suit! This man was spending money like he was going to die next week. He didn't want there to be anything left over for anyone to get.

"You're kidding right?" I asked him. "You don't come home to show your wife some suit just bought at Saks for eleven-hundred dollars, and expect her to be OK with it! Unless you're the Trumps. Take it back!"

"I deserve this suit," he said, trying to convince me.

"Do you know how many herbs we can buy to keep you well with that money? That's a month and a half rent in the rental house, or the mortgage payment on our new home. Take it back!"

"You can forget that, because after all I've been through, I deserve this new suit," he lamented.

I tried another angle. "If Franklin can make this suit identically, will you take it back?"

He eyed the suit. "Franklin can't make stuff this well, it came from Saks." I threw my hands up. Duke's advice resounded in my head, *don't be logical with illogical people.*

Steven decided he wasn't going to speak to me for whatever reason he made such a decision. And he chose to sleep on the couch in the office. This went on for two weeks. Every time I tried to talk to him, he'd say to me, "I'm not talking to you. I don't hear you." Was this a marriage or grade school?

"It's been more than a week since you haven't spoken to me. How long do you think you can live in the same house without speaking to someone?"

He finally had a real answer, "I didn't speak to my sister once for three months."

"Well, I ain't your sister, so if you don't want to respect me as your wife, I won't be one." I went on strike.

I stopped washing his clothes, cooking, and I didn't bother to clean the office where he chose to sleep. When it got to the point when we needed to talk about things regarding our move and he didn't want to, I started collecting boxes for my own things.

My Chicago buddy, transplanted in New York like me, Terria, came over during our silent feud. Steven was having a non-verbal tirade, stomping up and down the stairs, slamming doors, throwing things around. He was always selective about to whom he would show his true colors and Terria was a frequent recipient. She and I lounged on my bed talking when I asked her to pass my purse.

"Girlie, I don't know how you stay here with him, when he's so mean to you." Her arm dropped at the unexpected weight of it, "What in the world do you have in there?"

"You know what they say about us Chicago women, that we come packing," I told her of the old Chi-town folklore as I let her get a peek at my gun.

Terria was totally shocked, "Why do you have that?!!!!"

"Just in case Steven wants to find out what being from the South Side of Chicago really means. Let him keep acting crazy with me, and AIDS won't be what kills him."

Years later, Terria confided that experience left her traumatized and for my actions I truly apologize.

I packed my dishes, records and clothes and called Dewanda over to disconnect my computer. She cried the whole time. Then I called two friends: Ellen to drive me to the Poconos, and Garfield to help load boxes for the move.

Steve screamed at me for moving the computer. "I bought that computer with my mother's money, you leave it here. It's mine!"

I quietly left the box and came back with five thousand dollars cash placed it on the table in front of him, and I packed up the computer. While he was running all over town spending his money, I was saving mine.

I wanted to move on a Wednesday during the day while Steve was at work, but Garfield called to say that he was in the Bahamas and asked if I could wait until he returned on Friday. Ellen came straight to Brooklyn in her truck with boxes so we could roll out.

"I had a talk with Steven," she said as I folded my clothes and put them in boxes.

"Oh yeah, Steven, you mean he speaks?" she laughed.

"He told me everything," she said somberly sitting on the bed.

"Everything?" I quizzed with a raised eyebrow.

"Yes, everything."

I went in for the jugular. "Did he tell you he has AIDS?"

When she gasped, I knew he hadn't told that little detail.

"No he didn't tell me that, but he did tell me how much he loves you and that he doesn't want you to go."

"Then he can tell me himself," I said unfazed.

In the wee hours of the morning on my moving day, I felt the covers snatched off of me and Steven climbed into bed crying hysterically for me not to leave. Part of his behavior was also due to him not wanting to move to the Poconos after all.

"Steven, you can live where ever you want. LaJoyce is moving to the Poconos."

"Then I guess we're moving together. I love you too much to let you go," he pleaded.

"I do love you, but not at the expense of my emotional health. I can turn it off or on just like that," I said with a snap. "I told you to quit trying me, I ain't your sisters. I'm your wife and you should treat me with more respect than you have."

"I'm sorry."

"How many women do you know who would have stayed around once they got the news about your condition?" I asked. "I need you to be clear that wanting to move out had nothing to do with your diagnosis, but everything to do with your attitude."

"I'll do better," he promised.

"OK then, I'll tell Ellen I'm not going."

At Bible study that evening, Steve told everyone, "I almost didn't come up here tonight, but I didn't let the devil win."

Everyone shouted their hallelujah praises for Steven's about-face. There sat my closest friends, and they all knew the deal.

We moved into our rental house over the Fourth of July weekend and it was 107 degrees in the shade of the Pocono Mountains! I organized us in the house posthaste because I had to take a road trip the following weekend to my college campus, Eastern Illinois University in Charleston, Illinois for our Black Student Reunion. My former roomie Angela and I did a presentation called AIDS 101: Issues for People of Color. Angela was a serious sister who was an AIDS educator for the Department of Health, training the Chicago Police Department on every facet of AIDS.

We marveled how we had both come across this line of work helping others through this crisis. She and I rented a car to drive to Chicago after the reunion and while she slept, I cried like a baby up Interstate 57 North, toiling about how I should tell her that the AIDS epidemic had hit my home as well. Angela and I shared the deepest of secrets as college roomies do. This was something so close to us both and closer than she had ever imagined.

I decided that for one weekend, I'd be free of such cumbersome conversation. I wanted for a moment to enjoy my friend and my freedom. I didn't want to shed any tears, to give any back-stories, or to get any sympathy. I was totally the LaJoyce that Angela remembered. She and I vowed we'd be friends for life. I didn't want her to know that life had shown up front and center in the form of AIDS.

When I returned home from that trip Steven announced, "I'm buying a dog today and I don't care what you say."

"Why has got it to be all like that, I love dogs. See there, you're expecting a positive thing to be a negative. Stop it!," I warned.

The most adorable white German shepherd puppy came to live with us. I named her Missy in honor of the German shepherd my Grannie once owned. Missy immediately became my dog. This drove Steven to purchase a dog "just for me," he said - - a Rottweiler we named Rambo.

Soon after we moved to the Poconos and broke ground on our home, Steven was down-sized as the assistant parts manager for the BMW dealership where he worked. It was only about two weeks before he got another position at a luxury parts sales company in central New Jersey. I had gone to work for Patti at her public relations company in Somerville, New Jersey. We began car-pooling, with him dropping me off first.

It was just in the nick of time that Steven didn't have to go to the city anymore. His temperament was unable to handle the New York City traffic any longer. It seemed as though every day, he'd have a road rage experience. In one episode on the way to Queens to visit Uncle Charles, a guy in the other car literally scraped the my side of the car. At the next light, I got out in the middle of the street and took the subway home to Brooklyn.

Steven was preoccupied with death ever since his diagnosis. He said he always felt that he wouldn't live to be 33 years old. It was as a result of some freaky recurring dream he had, so he said.

The night before his 33rd birthday, he refused to go to sleep. I promised him I'd stay awake, but in true fashion I fell asleep at 9:30. When I awoke at 4 a.m. and found him sleeping. I shook him awake to let him know he was still breathing. He was so happy, and I for him, that we had sex – with a rubber – right then.

He was constantly exhibiting classic death wish behavior, so his acting out with his car and in other places let me know that although he was blessed to still be in the game of life, he did not know how to play. For the game of life and how to play it is with God before you.

We moved into our newly built home on my birthday weekend of September 1994! But not before our Pastor K.P. came to pray in every room before any furniture went in it. I had been introduced to the church by Ellen and I never missed a Tuesday night Bible study and my boldness in the Lord increased even more under this ministry. Steven liked to attend occasionally on Sundays. What we enjoyed most was fellowship with our prophetic, anointed and crazy new Pastor K.P.

Steven had taken ill after the Saturday portion of the move with our local friends. On Sunday, I had to do all of the moving with the friends who had came to lend a hand. In my opinion, Steven was running game on being ill so that he couldn't help. He didn't like the crew I had called in, three of my gay friends.

"Why you gotta call them? You know how I feel. I just want to do the move and get it over with. I hope they aren't spending the night! I don't want them in my house overnight," he shouted angrily.

He didn't want them in his house overnight now, but when we had the three of them up with Dewanda and Lucy one weekend, the gay crew took over and did all of the cooking and brought all of the food for the mountain festivities. Dewanda remembered later that Steven took Missy, left us at home and was gone until nightfall. He said he'd gone to our property for the new house and he got lost in the woods. Dewanda said it sounded strange to her then, but never said anything.

So he chose to play the avoidance game, pretending to be sick on the final day of our move. I had to ask God's forgiveness on that one for real. My anger was creeping dangerously in Steven's direction with all of the crap he was pulling. Without the AIDS diagnosis, his behavior was enough to make anyone want to pop him in the face on a regular basis. Now compound that with AIDS, and it was a potentially lethal combination.

Steven was coming down with bouts of dementia. Sometimes he was totally lucid and other times he was as nutty as a fruit cake. Because of his pre-existing health condition, we could not garner any additional life insurance on him. I signed up for credit life insurance on the house, but that just covered me. For my physical exam for the house, the insurance company sends a nurse to your door and you must present photo identification. Steven wanted to ask Stacey to pose as him so that we'd be able to get credit life.

"Honey, that's insurance fraud!" I told him.

"But you are not going to get much insurance money. At least the house will be paid off when I die. I'll ask Stacey, he will do it for me."

"How can you go to sleep at night conjuring up such mess? It's not fair for you to ask your best friend to commit insurance fraud for you."

"I guess you're right."

"You better not ask him, Steven."

"OK, OK, I won't," he conceded.

Years later, when we were discussing this, Stacey and Claudette exchanged glances knowingly because Steven called him after all behind my back and asked him to commit the crime. I thought, *Some best friend, huh?*

Fortunately, I had my work to keep me busy. Patti had an awesome client roster with Stephanie Mills, George Howard, Levert, and The O'Jay's. Patti turned George Howard over to me, because he had been a thorn in the side of GRP Records when it came to press.

My job: Mend old broken relationships with media outlets, and get George to see he was a star.

I threw everything I had into George including the kitchen sink, taking him fresh baked goodies on our first meeting. I started calling him GH after that and he became a media darling nationwide. We talked so much that we ended up calling one another brother and sister. Then at a family gathering, we discovered we were related, very, very distantly, but related nonetheless. Not only was he a relative but he was also my best friend, next to Tyger that is. I even tried to hook them up when he got divorced!

Steve loved George Howard's jazzy saxophone music and he played it all of the time on the shows he produced for Vaughn Harper. Because he liked GH's music so much, he was tolerant of when I had to go into the city to be with him, or on a road trip.

One day in October 1994, right in the middle of our work day, Steven appeared at the office door, allowing it to hold him up, "Rabbit, I'm sick, you gotta take me to the hospital."

All conversations ceased. Patti hung up the phone mid-conversation and put her shoes on, I followed suit. We had to help him down the stairs. He had just driven me here less than 3 hours ago, how did he get so sick so fast? I thought.

With the condition he was in and considering our proximity to the Poconos, we needed to get to an emergency room.

Patti drove us to the JFK Medical Center in nearby Metuchen, New Jersey, where Steven was placed in a sterile room. He was diagnosed with PCP Pneumonia - again. Upon entering his room you had to don a gown, gloves, head and shoe coverings, and a face mask. There was absolutely no spending the night in there, it was treated like an intensive care unit but with private rooms.

I spent many nights on the couch in the living room at Patti's house during the week, so I could already be at work. Her family was wonderful in extending their hospitality to me while I balanced Steve, work, and my Pocono household. I had identified teenagers Jelani and Gyasi as neighborhood dog walkers for Missy and Rambo and during the week I went home on Wednesdays and Fridays. Steve stayed at JFK for a month.

His doctor advised that Steven was going to be officially put on permanent disability. *Wow, I have a disabled husband*, I thought. It was easier to deal with when he was feeling good and not looking sick. I had to start my Florence Nightingale role all over again. We knew what to do. I'd done this all before and he got well. God said, *"Hold on and don't let go."*

What I didn't know how to manage was my mounting emotional stress and the system that we were being thrown into. When I went to Social Services to apply for food stamps, the case worker said that Steven himself had to apply in person.

"But Miss, he can't sit up in a car. Do you make house calls?" I wanted to know.

"You have to bring him here and I have to see that he is alive and a real person. I'm sorry but people have abused the system to the point that this is how we have to do it now."

I made an appointment for two days later and carted Steven to the truck, laid him down on a palette, and drove to the next town so the lady could *see* him. Her face was ashen when she looked at this sick cavern of a man who was just 33 years old. She gave me a sympathetic look. I hated it when people looked at me like that. It was my new reality and I needed to deal with it.

Meanwhile, we were sinking financially. As much as I liked working with Patti, I needed to find another job. I made sure I paid the mortgage first, while I did a juggling act to keep everything else in the air. I had us on payment plans with everyone from the man who delivers the wood to the phone company. Steven discussed bankruptcy for himself, but first he wanted to charge his credit cards up to the hock. I didn't like that idea at all.

The next day, the lady from Social Services called to say we were denied food stamps because Steven's disability check from New Jersey was one hundred dollars too much. I understood why people cheated the system. When you needed it most, nothing was there. I needed another job fast.

My parents came for Christmas along with my brother Stevie and his son Cory. It was their first time seeing the new house. Mommie was totally into decorating the windows and decking the halls with boughs of holly.

Steven loved Christmas but he was battling a slight fever for a couple of days. Fevers were the measuring point of infection. He refused to take the infection medication but he asked me to whip up an herbal remedy instead. I felt we should go to the hospital, because he was still cold with the heat on 90 and several comforters. I knew the last thing he wanted to do was go to the hospital on Christmas Eve, but I was willing if necessary. Fortunately his temperature only went up to 100 that night and he slept well.

On Christmas morning, I heard the headboard banging in my bedroom. I ran upstairs to look, and from the doorway I shouted downstairs, "Call 911! Steven is having a seizure!" I grabbed his hands so he wouldn't hurt himself.

In our community we have an internal paramedic unit that is dispatched within minutes of calling 911. Mr. Frailey, our neighbor, was at the door in 5 minutes arriving just after Steven's second seizure. Mr. Frailey was retired from the Pocono Medical Center and it was rumored that he was most awesome. I witnessed it first hand, when he put his fingers on Steven's cheek and belted out, "104.5!"

When the paramedics from town got there, sure enough the fever was 104.5. I thought of Mr. Frailey, *"He's my own personal angel right here."* I stepped into the hall to speak with the paramedics and Steven began seizing again, number three. After he was stabilized, it was clear they needed to strap him to a gurney and get to the hospital. I was crying a steady stream of tears. Mommie held my hand. Just as the paramedics got to the door with him, he had another seizure, number four!

Bo Daddy and I followed the ambulance to Pocono Medical Center. Steven was admitted on Christmas Day. Wasn't it just like Jesus to arrange His special day so that you could show His love by taking care of someone else? Steven was totally in a catatonic state. He had a collapsed lung as a result of the recent pneumonia and all of that seizing also contributed.

"It will be a miracle if he makes it through the next 48 hours," the doctors said.

I wanted Steven to hold on, there were things that I knew he needed to get right with his sisters before he checked out of here. We stayed in his room a while, but he was barely there. The doctors said that was a side effect of so many consecutive grand seizures accompanied by a high fever. There was nothing we could do but wait it out and it was best to do that at home.

Two days later, Steven snapped out of his catatonic state enough to give me specific instructions, "I'm thinking about going bankrupt for real now. I want you to go and run-up the credit cards. Get everything we want."

"Seriously?" I didn't have time to do such a thing, nor did I think it was right.

He started making out a list, "Take Mommie shopping because she's been here through all of my crises and Bo too."

Bo Daddy piped up, "Nah, we don't need nothing."

Make sure you do something good for Fabia, I'm so proud of her." Fabia is Uncle Charles' daughter, who was an undergrad at Colgate University on a scholarship and headed to law school at Villanova, again on scholarship. We were all proud of our Fabia. As he sat there making out his wish list, I have to admit I got caught up in the excitement. I hadn't bought myself anything in quite sometime.

I wasn't much of a shopper because growing up, Mommie took us shopping with her every day. EVERY day. To this day, shopping is a necessity for me. "Steven are you sure?" I asked again.

"Do it," he said.

"OK, I'll start tomorrow."

CHAPTER SIX

The Realization of the Truth

"And ye shall know the truth, and the truth shall make you free."
John 8:32

Stevie, Cory and I hit the malls early and stayed there all day. It was very hard for me to spend money like that. There was no joy in it but definitely a fever that we all got caught up in. When I ran out of ideas of things to buy, I'd just walk into a store and ask for a few hundred dollars of gift certificates. I couldn't believe I didn't really know what to buy.

Stevie got stuff to fix up the basement. That would be one thing Steven would love when he got home. When his sisters came, they were presented with very lovely things as well as gift certificates. As promised, Fabia was also taken shopping.

A very interesting thing happened on the second day of the shopping spree, the number 24 kept appearing everywhere. It was 24 past the hour every time I looked. The counter on the tape player would be on 24, the change I had to pay at the store would be 24, the change I would receive would be 24. The number had always been significant for me because it is the date of my birthday. At first I thought that is all it was, but I remembered a preacher somewhere saying that if you keep seeing a number, it doesn't mean for you to run out and play that number. It means for you to look up that Psalm because there is a message for you. I made a mental note to read Psalm 24 when I got home.

We visited Steven who was sleeping soundly by the time we got to the hospital and I woke him to let him know I was there. The first thing he wanted to know was, did I go shopping? I nodded.

"Good," he said turning his head, "Go home, Rabbit, and get some sleep." I followed his instruction, plus I was exhausted from all of that shopping.

I told Mommie and Bo Daddy that I was going to take a bath and go to sleep. Just as I crawled into the bed and was about to turn off the TV, the doctor called to say I needed to come back to the hospital right away to sign papers for Steven to get a blood transfusion or he wouldn't make it through the night.

"I'm on my way," I said. "Lord, what is all of this?"

Just as I was going to turn off the TV to get dressed, I hit the time button on the remote instead. It said 10:24! That reminded me, read Psalms 24. I grabbed my Bible - - it would only take a minute:

The earth is the Lord's, and the fullness thereof; the world, and they that dwell therein,

For he hath founded it upon the seas, and established it upon the floods,

Who shall ascend into the hill of the Lord? Or who shall stand in his holy place?

He that hath clean hands, and a pure heart; who hath not lifted up his soul unto vanity, nor sworn deceitfully.

He shall receive the blessing from the Lord, and righteousness from the God of his salvation.

This is the generation of them that seek him, that seek thy face, O Jacob, Selah,

Lift up your heads, O ye gates; and be ye lift up, ye everlasting doors; and the King of glory shall come in.

Who is this King of glory? The Lord strong and mighty, the Lord mighty in battle.

Lift up your heads, O ye gates; even lift them up, ye everlasting doors and the King of glory shall come in.

Who is this King of glory? The Lord of hosts, he is the King of glory. Selah.

I closed the Bible to get up to leave and the Spirit said, *"Wait a minute! Meditate on that."*

I remembered singing the song "Lift Up Your Heads O, Ye Gates" in the children's choir. The music flooded my memory. Then I opened the Bible again and my eyes fell on:

Who shall ascend into the hill of the Lord? Or who shall stand in his holy place?

He that hath clean hands, and a pure heart.

Then it hit me, this was about Steve. The scripture asks this with a question mark. He was the only one who at that moment, whom I knew would soon make his ascent into the hill of the Lord and to stand in his Holy place. The scripture went on to answer the very question it asked. And the answer was:

He that hath clean hands, and a pure heart...

"Wasn't Steven's heart pure? Weren't his hands clean?" I asked aloud to myself.

The Holy Spirit told me, *"get the medical records."* I reached into the bottom of Steven's nightstand for the 400 dollars' worth of medical records from Mercy Hospital. I started from the back, not knowing what I was searching for.

The Holy Spirit told me, *"start from the beginning."*

It was there I saw it. On the very first day Steven had gone to Mercy Hospital, it was written "Patient confirms he has HIV."

My body went numb, "Hold up!" I said out loud, "Hold up!" I read those handwritten words again. They knew from the first day he went to the hospital!? A million questions ran through my mind, why didn't they tell me on day one? Why would they make me wait 40 days?! I can't believe a doctor would not tell a wife her own husband has AIDS – I answered that one on my own: policy.

I read the handwritten words again and then I saw even more clearly the words: "patient confirms."

That means Steven TOLD them he had AIDS. That means he knew! He knew all along he had HIV. I was so dumbfounded, I just sat staring at the blank white wall in my room. Then right before my eyes, God replayed for me everything He had tried to show me but I refused to see.

It started with the first day I met him, when Steven said he was in the hospital for bleeding ulcers. That was lie number one. He didn't even know me a half hour before he started lying to me. He knew he had HIV and chose to have unprotected sex with me! He could have let me choose. He took away my freedom of choice in making the decision to be with him or not in spite of his disease.

This also meant he didn't do this by himself, he had help in his mother. The movie continued to play...

Mama Mo saying, "Don't wait on money to get married." And, "I'll send you on a honeymoon for 15 days." And asking my parents for money because "you'll never get this opportunity again to go to Hawaii." And paying for an abortion.

Well, I'll be daggone. Since they were choosing to be in denial about Steven having AIDS, they were also uneducated about the disease to the point that when I got pregnant, they thought there would also be an AIDS-infected baby. Not knowing that if the mother is negative, then the baby is absolutely negative. So now they've got the blood of an innocent baby on their hands. I hope she asked forgiveness from God like I had. Her motivation seemed entirely different than mine, it was all in the name of this secret they were harboring. A deadly secret.

The movie on the wall played the wedding:

Me before - - "I've got the strangest feeling I shouldn't be doing this."

The oldest sister - - "You just don't know, you're taking a lot off our hands, chile."

The youngest sister - - "He's your problem now, don't send him back to our house.

Mama Mo - - "See Steven, I told you about all that worrying, everything always works out in the end." Wink, wink.

"Whaaaaat!" I said crying, "they all knew! Everyone knew but me?" Eleven months of dating, two years of marriage, and lots of sex - - funny, he never mentioned it.

The movie kept playing...

Steven spending money like a man who would never have any more. Steven wanting to take a bath before going to the hospital, because he knew he wasn't coming back. His oldest sister saying she knew he had AIDS when he made the announcement. Steven being sure that I was sick too. Steven not being sure where he got the disease - - or deeper yet, not willing to *admit* where he got the disease. All of the disappearing acts he pulled over the years played out. And finally the night of the fire when he fell to his knees asking, "Now, who am I going to tell all of my secrets to!"

I was numb sitting on the edge of my bed digesting all this. One thing was for sure, there was NO way I was going to go down to that hospital to sign any papers for a blood transfusion. He'd just have to die before morning.

I started talking to God, "Help me make some sense of this?" God had already showed me what He had been trying to tell me. But no, I was so busy worrying about not having a husband at age 28 and planning my wedding, that I refused to see things put right in my face. I also was in direct violation of the Word by going out to find a "good man."

The Bible is very clear in Proverbs 18:22, it says;

"He who finds a wife, findeth a good thing."

It does **Not** say, <u>she</u> who finds a man finds a good thing.

I had to praise the Lord for keeping me through all of my stupidity. I was just like the little kid who kept saying, "Daddy please, Daddy please." Until, finally Daddy just said, "Here!"

I repented for being disobedient. I know that delayed obedience is disobedience. "Lord, right now I have the power of Steven's life tonight in my hands."

I could have very easily laid down, fallen asleep and conveniently forgotten about going to the hospital. I could have run to show everyone the medical records that had the documentation of what he had done. I could have taken that piece of evidence to the police and had him arrested for attempted murder. And I could have taken the wedding video to the police also and brought both sisters up on the same charges and added conspiracy to boot. Or I could just show the medical records to my brother downstairs and he'd call for reinforcement from my other brothers in Chicago and they'd be here by morning - - not a pretty sight.

"What am I going to get Lord if I do the right thing here and now? I need you to tell me how am I going to benefit from, once again taking the high road? For once I'm asking, what are you going to do for LaJoyce? And please don't take all night to answer me, I need to know right now. Or tonight, Steven is a dead man."

God had never been more clear to me than at that very moment, *"Vengeance is mine, I've got this. Stand still and I will bless you. Don't tell anyone tonight about your discovery. Leave now."*

I wiped my face, put on clothes, went downstairs and asked Bo Daddy to ride with me. I signed the papers at the hospital and they said they thought I wasn't coming. The doctor was just about to call me again when I arrived. I didn't want to go into Steven's room. I just signed and left.

Back in my room, I thanked God for His promise and I whole-heartedly forgave Steven. He had to have been a fool for trying to do-in a Child of the King. I needed to forgive him because he had no clue that I was God's Girl – for real.

I thanked God for keeping me. Quite simply, it was nothing but the blood of Jesus keeping me covered, in a negative HIV status and safe from hurt, harm and danger. I sang myself to sleep:

"As I walk through the storm, hold your head up high. And don't be afraid of the dark...."

Steven spent another four weeks in the hospital and they thought it was quite miraculous that he left there alive. By the time he got home, my emotions about the truth were settled. There were going to be some changes around here. My brother Stevie stayed after

Mommie and Bo left to help me around the house and to lend a hand for when Steven finally came home.

It turns out that while Steven was in the hospital barking out orders to make this purchase and that, he was in the midst one of his demented episodes. He would swing back and forth between periods of lucid behavior. When he got home and started going through the mail, he flipped out when he saw the credit card bills. I mean flipped!

He cussed me out for shopping and buying stuff for the house. He got on the phone and called everyone in his family to report that I was trying to kill him early by bringing all of this financial stress on him. Here's the kicker: he never even *remembered* telling me that he was going to file bankruptcy and to go shopping.

"That's a joke. Why would I do that so some other nigger can come up in here when I'm gone and you all laugh at me for being a sucker while you enjoy this stuff you bought," he fumed. "Why would I want to make life easy for you when I'm gone!"

"You told me to do this!"

"It wasn't a done deal. You should have never done it."

I was beginning to see clearly now. All too clearly. Either Steven was truly going through bouts of dementia or he had serious game. I chalked it up to both in light of my newfound truth.

He said, "I need to get away from you. I don't have that much time left and I don't want to be here in this cold. I want to go out to California with my Godmother and die out there where it's warm."

"Really? And what about your doctor's appointments? And who's going to take care of you?" I asked him, concerned because Godmother Martha was a nurse, didn't mean she could do what I do with all of my concoctions.

"They'll do a better job than you, cause these bills are causing me nothing but stress," he said flinging the bills in my face. "Now where's the fur coat you bought."

"It's still at the shop," I told him.

"Well, return it!" he screamed.

"I'll be returning every single thing I bought. See, I didn't want to do this in the first place, but nooooo, you wanted me to get this and that. So I tell you what, I'll take it all back, gift certificates included. Cause it ain't nothing but stuff to me."

"I told everybody in my family what you did."

"Good, now you can tell them I returned it all," I shouted as I started gathering things to put near the front door including all of the gift certificates. "Never mind, I'll tell them myself!" I stomped upstairs, slammed the door and went to bed.

He must have stayed up all night talking to my brother and even after Stevie went to sleep, because there was not one gift certificate to be found in the house when I woke up. To this day, I don't know to whom he gave so many gift certificates. There were only a handful of people coming to the house regularly. Claudette and Stacey said that it wasn't to them, so I still have no idea.

I knew about these types of episodes, and it was my fault for not realizing the dementia in him sooner. It was very sad at seeing him slowly lose his motor skills, by flipping over in our truck, totaling it – to watching him lose his mental capacity, it was killing me deep down.

I wrote the family this following letter of apology:

31 January 1995

Dear Family:

It's ironic I write a letter on this day, Steven and I met this very day in 1990. By now I'm sure you all know what I have done recently that has caused Steven a great deal of stress. I am writing to say to all of you that I never in a million years intended to hurt him and to say that I'm sorry.

My rationale for doing these things is not elementary at all. It goes beyond my being selfish, which is just the emotion/action that is on the surface. But what is really underneath is a severe panic, fear, loneliness. You all are not intimate as I am with what is going on with him and the disease. I'm now well read on the subject and I should have noticed this end-stage dementia before I went shopping.

I've seen you all recently and you've commented on my strength during this ordeal. I guess I've got you all fooled because that is the biggest facade imaginable. That strength characteristic is a face I put on every day to make it. I put on strength so I don't break down and cry, kick, scream and holler in front of Steven and have him to worry even more. So I do my crying each time I leave this house in the car. I break down in public places. I excuse myself from my desk daily to run to the bathroom or I sit there staring out of the window, tears streaming, hoping no one sees me "doing that again."

So what do I do? I tell all of you and even others that I'm doing OK and not to worry. When that is a lie above all lies. But what do I really say? Do I share the litany that I live daily? Can I really scream out loud to say how much this is too killing me. So I say all is well. Not just to you all but to everybody. So when it finally came down to me cracking up, I didn't jump up and down, I didn't warn anybody, I didn't run off for days unable to be found, I didn't go jump in the sack with some stranger to ease my pain. I went shopping after I was told to go by Steven.

Steven says that I had to have put a lot of thought into where I went to make those kinds of purchases. But I will tell you that is not true. I simply got in the car and started driving and charged wherever I landed. For a period of a week and a half I know I went completely crazy. I thought Steven would be pleased by having the basement fixed so I took care of that first. Because even though the doctors were saying he wasn't coming home after five seizures and a collapsed lung, I knew he was.

Even though he had discussed bankruptcy, nothing was final yet. I rationalized the buying like everything was approved and a done deal. He says I didn't cover my tracks very well. That's because I wasn't trying to sneak. I'm not a good liar. Never have been. I've never been sneaky. My eyes reveal too much.

So from that time, to the time Steven got the bills in the mail, I was a nervous wreck. If I would have been in a right state in the first place I would have never bought one thing to add to the pressures of what we deal with here daily. It was an intermittent escape. That's the best way I can describe the feeling at the time.

Escapade completed. Reality still here, and back to my daily routine as follows: get in car and cry all the way to work and home; be scared to come in the house because I don't know if Steven will be in here dead or not; cry because you go to sleep one day and the next your whole life is turned upside down; fight with Social Services about why we can't get food stamps, cash assistance or Medicaid even though we've worked our entire lives; go to doctor's appointments and listen to them tell me Steven doesn't have long; write letters to creditors about Steven's disability to ask for reduction in monthly payments; cry about Steven's immobility, face breakouts, lack of appetite, dementia, shrinking frame; coordinate neighbors to check in so he won't be here alone all day; guard his privacy - keep straight in my head who knows who doesn't know; help him go to the bathroom; making the bed finding blood-stained sheets; call doctor because blood is a problem; don't forget latex gloves wash blood-stained stuff separately, bleach first; cry, that in sickness and in health stuff is for real; pay a few bills- mortgage first; look for a job; go to an interview; grocery shop-don't forget chocolate milk and cinnamon pop tarts, it's the only thing I can count on Steven consuming; wash his hair; check in on him in middle of the night - temperature may get too high, he still insists on sleeping with the heat blaring; cry, because he's always cold; order more wood, pick up more coal, call electric company, make payment arrangements the bill is $800!!!; feed Missy and Rambo; pay neighbor to feed and walk them after school, Steven is too weak; cry, the dogs are his pride but he can't really enjoy them; love him so much wish I could take some of the pain; cry because I know I can't; chase down station wagon car payment from source, convinced it was a bad business deal but we can't pay so better late than never; cry because I need to get a better paying job to help rescue us from the system that we can't get into anyhow and to get the best doctors without having to worry about how to pay the bill; go to Brooklyn twice a month to get $200 medicine for free; medical bills can't pay; other bills use them to start the fires in the wood-burning stove; cry, bill collectors calling from 8 a.m. to10 p.m. getting on my nerves; get a new phone number; cry, there are a lot of people we will never remember to call to give them the new number; have to go on a business trip, I hate to leave Steven alone; call home, machine picks up, mind races cry myself into an almost sleep, race home relieved he's still here; cry, he talks about the strangest things, about wanting his mother, how she will make everything all right and take care of him; concentrate, begin on next book; cry, want to write about these emotions but I don't want anybody to see what I'm feeling; maybe an article about our situation would help some people, can't do it-need to guard his privacy; go to post office, sign for certified letters, getting hauled into court for not paying a contractor; cry, money/bills stress Steven; need to go to church or Bible study, can't, don't want to leave Steven alone-pray at home, watch the preachers on TV and read my Bible; looking forward to nephews Robbie and Cory's visit for the holidays; cry, no kids of our own; get up at 6 a.m. clean wood and coal stoves, dump in more coal, start fire, wash dishes, put in a load of clothes, make lunch for Steven, label and leave in fridge, feed and take out dogs, bathe, get dressed, get in the car and cry.

These are just a few of the emotions that are locked up under the "I'm doing OK" facade. We've got two choices here and that is to deal or to deny. I'm trying to deal. I broke down for a period and now I'm back and returning the purchases.

God forgives me, I hope you will too.

Love you all...LaJoyce

Steven was flabbergasted that I actually sent a letter to his sisters, Uncle, Godmother and cousins. I told him, "Let's see who returns those gift certificates you passed out. You wanna tell everyone our business, let's tell it ALL. Why do they only get to hear your story? You do realize I have a story in all of this, too?"

Uncle Charles was the only one who called me to say anything about it. "I'm praying for you," he said earnestly. For me, that was all he needed to say and it sealed our relationship forever.

When Stevie left to return to Chicago, he gave me a gun tour in my own house. He said he watched Steven look at a gun in the office one night and then hide it. "I figured that chump had a gun hidden in every room of this house, and I was right. You be careful, and let me show you the new places every room has a gun," Stevie said showing me the hiding places. He was tearful when leaving and let me know he could be here by car in ten hours any time of day or night. "Just call."

Stevie was absolutely on target to move those guns away from Steven. Two days later he said, "I think that little brother of yours was stealing from us while he was here."

"Really, what's missing?" I asked, thinking he discovered something other than guns missing for real.

"I don't know yet, but I bet he took something."

"Let me know what's missing and I'll tell Mommie to take it out of his behind!" I said to him.

Later that night, I took a peek at all of the new hiding places and all guns were still nicely tucked away where my little brother had left them. I just let Steven continue to think that Stevie stole the guns from our home. He didn't mention it, and neither did I.

In the middle of the Pocono winter, Steven left home one day in the truck and called me later that night to say he was in Long Island and would be staying with his sisters for two weeks because he needed to get away from me.

"OK, make sure they do everything for you that I do," I said to make sure he would stay well.

"Oh, they will," he assured. *Mmmmmm*, I thought, *suddenly they were all getting along and were going to take care of him*? When did this occurrence appear since we began this vicious merry-go-round with hospitals and doctors? I could count how many times they came to visit. Never once bringing a bag of groceries, a prepared meal, or offering respite to me. Instead, they'd bounce in from the Long Island haul – and the three-hour trip was a haul – hungry and ravaging my pots and refrigerator, leaving a dirty kitchen and dishes in their quake. So I needed to be forgiven if I was wrong about them taking good care of him all of a sudden, when because of their glaring absence, they didn't even know how to care for him in this condition.

"If you wanted to spend time with your sisters, I would have taken you out there. Why did you drive out there by yourself?" I questioned him because it was very obvious he was a candidate to have his license revoked due to health issues.

"Cause of what you did, I couldn't stand looking at you another day."

"Whatever Steven. You may not remember telling me to shop, but I have Stevie, Bo Daddy, and little Cory to corroborate with me. And I bet I can find a nurse or two who heard you giving me a shopping list. Don't forget you were 30 thousand dollars in debt when I met you, that *we* have been paying since we got married. You've barely made a dent in that. The 20 thousand dollars I've just spent is not only returnable, but a joke compared to the debt you already had. They can all vouch for the fact that you appeared to be lucid at the time you told me to go!"

"There you go using big words, what's lucid ?" he asked irritated.

"If you're well enough to drive three hours to Long Island, then pick up a dictionary." Steven hated to read and never even bothered to read one pamphlet about his illness. I did all of the reading and researching.

I had started to think that he was running game with me about the degree of his weakness. Here's a shell of a man, who claimed he could barely walk, let alone pack the largest suitcase in the house and make a three-hour trip. I seriously wondered.

He had ordered me to come out there that weekend with items he needed to take to California.

"I'll drive the Honda out and switch for the truck when I get there," I advised.

"No, you won't. I told my sister she could drive the truck while I was gone."

"Whaaat? And what am I supposed to drive when it snows and I can't get off of the mountain to get to work to *pay* for the truck *she's* driving? What exactly am I supposed to do then?" I questioned.

"Whatever you have to, but the truck stays here."

I had a huge concert event with George Howard that weekend in the city and in Long Island at Westbury Music Fair. GH was on a Smooth Jazz tour with Grover Washington, Jr., Phil Perry, and Dianne Reeves and they were killing audiences all around the country. When GH saw me, he knew I was totally stressed because I had lost a considerable amount of weight.

GH took my face in his hands and his eyes welled-up, "You can hide it over the phone baby sis, but you can't hide it in front of me any longer. What's up?" He knew Steven was sick, but he had the stomach cancer story.

"I'll tell you later," I answered looking around at all of the people backstage.

"Stop playing, you'll tell me now," he said, concerned, and turned me his ear. I whispered the truth. He covered his face and cried right backstage at Westbury Music Fair. We hugged and I assured him that I was definitely negative, and my weight loss was indeed from stress. My photographer for the evening, Ronnie Wright, saw us huddled and told us to smile. I have the most beautiful photo of us with GH's watery eyes.

I spent the night with his sisters at the house they were renting. With all of the money they got between the two of them, instead of pooling it toward ownership, they chose to rent. Go figure. One look in their refrigerator and I knew Steven was not being fed the right way. There was a load of chocolate milk, and bananas. There was no other fruit and no salad fixin's so I knew he hadn't eaten any. I had brought groceries of the things he needed to eat and bags of herbs I had pre-mixed so they had to just add hot water.

Steven was pulling a not-speaking-to-me episode that weekend. It took so much more effort to be nasty than it did to be nice.

Before leaving on Sunday, I gave him an egg facial because his face was all broken out. I told him while he had his mask on and couldn't talk back, "I'm glad to see that you and your sisters are speaking. Please patch up all the way and discuss everything you want to talk about that has had you angry. And I hope you're not here just because you're angry with me."

He may have been mad with me, but he didn't pass up the pampering session for his facial. I told him I had brought enough herbs to take to California and supplements as well. I labeled everything and sent an instruction sheet.

The sisters just said, "We'll try. We don't have time to do all of this."

"I love you and have fun when you go to California. See you when you get back," I said.

"I told you I was going out there to die. I'm not coming back," he said adamantly.

I got a flash of the wedding video again as I left those siblings to themselves, "He's your problem now, don't send him back to our house."

At my home in the Poconos, there was an eerie peace that had enveloped it since Steven left. He had refused to speak to me on the phone and I didn't know what his exact travel plans were. I got a lot of rest and started looking for another job. I hated to leave the Patti fold but I needed more money, or we were going to lose everything. Having a dying husband was expensive! I was only writing five checks a month and it was tight.

I was on payment arrangements with everyone, and if the payment was not on time with the phone company, they would shut off the long distance service. I was diligent, but it happened. Patti didn't have enough money to pay us one Friday because a client didn't pay. I had already mailed the bills before coming to work that morning. Three days later, I only had incoming service. It was GH who came to my rescue. He allowed me to use his telephone credit card to make calls until I got myself straightened out.

Godmother Martha called me to let me know Steven had been there three days and that he was really weak, but she would take care of him. I knew that was gospel. While he was gone, I got myself back on track with church and Bible study and it felt good to be amongst my church family who had been praying for me.

In April 1995, my long-time industry friend Jackie called me up to let me know of an opening at Arista Records as publicity manager in New York City. I jumped at the chance. I didn't even know how much the salary was, but it didn't matter. I needed a job with benefits, because currently I didn't have any.

In my interview process, I had to tell them about my husband at home dying of stomach cancer. They needed to know he was in the final stages and when that time came for me to be near, I would have to be absent.

"No problem at all," my vice president said, visibly wrecked from the news. She even kissed me good-bye. She was also very impressed with the fact that I took the interview just off of the plane, with luggage in tow returning from a benefit GH held in Atlanta for the Clark-Atlanta University band.

"I knew I liked you, a woman who's not afraid to travel," she marveled.

When she told me the salary would be 35 thousand, I almost fell out my chair, because the week before at Bible study, Pastor K.P. delivered an awesome prophecy.

He interrupted the teaching, "If anyone can give 35 dollars right now, come up here and place it on the altar. I'm going to anoint your purse, your wallet... and in the next seven days, God is saying that he will increase you ten-fold, some of you one-hundred fold, some of you one-thousand fold."

I usually take issue with pastors who say give this to get that, but Pastor K.P. would dismiss church and forget to raise the offering and we'd all have to put our envelopes in a basket upon leaving. So, I knew it wasn't about "raising" money. What was interesting is that before coming to church I went to the store for fruit and veggies with only a 50 dollar bill. I asked the cashier for all fives back from my less-than-ten dollar purchase, and I didn't know why. I took that the I-don't-know-why feeling as a direct communication from God.

When Pastor K.P. made that call, I was amongst the first up to the altar. He told me, "Go get your purse." I brought up my backpack and he asked, "Is this where you keep your money?"

"Yes," I answered and the congregation laughed.

He ordered, "Don't laugh at her! If this is where she keeps her money, then this bag gets anointed!" My leather backpack got all greased up with blessed oil and I went praising all the way home. Approximately six days later, the 35 dollars was increased one-thousand fold. I just wished I had bought that tape!

After we sealed the Arista start date, I bounced onto West 57th Street and praised the Lord.

My new job was absolutely awesome! I was publicity manager and my roster included Craig Mack, Biggie Smalls –AKA- The Notorious B.I.G., his wife Faith Evans, Sean "Puffy" Combs (as he was known back then), Total, 112, OutKast, and Toni Braxton.

It was fast-paced to the nth power! I had an assistant named Samantha and she marveled how I juggled three phone lines simultaneously. When you receive 250 calls a day, there is no way you call anybody back. If someone calls you, put them on hold and get to them quickly. My first task was to plan a rap party happening in one week, for a DJ compilation CD. The only thing done for the event was identifying its location. I loved this work and I definitely needed the diversion.

I was summoned home to Chicago one weekend for a much-needed visit alone with my folks. All I did was sit in my room and stare out of my window, thinking... Mommie would come up to the room with a different beverage – juice, iced tea, or peach wine cooler. Depending on what she brought to drink, would be what kind of conversation we'd have.

Steven still wasn't speaking to me. Every time I called California, he would say he was tired and get off of the phone. Godmother Martha told me that I might want to consider coming out there to visit him, because she knew it was coming to the end.

Mommie and I did a lot of talking and thanking God about what He had done in my life. I know she just wanted to see her baby for a minute in her house. Grounding, is what you call it – returning to the point of safety. My grounding point was my room at Mommie's house.

Before leaving for church on Sunday, the Holy Spirit told me to get to Gus' house to pray for Daddy Brookshire, who had recently gone blind. I went there to lay hands on Daddy's eyes and pray for his healing.

"I have a surprise for you," Mama Brookshire said, dialing the phone. "Gus Brookshire's room please," she asked.

"Are they in town?" I wanted to know.

Mama Brookshire hesitated, "No..., well he...". I've known the Brookshire's most of my life from the neighborhood and Mama has never been one short of words. I knew something was wrong.

"My boy ain't washing no hair!" Daddy Brookshire piped up angrily.

"Wash hair? What is going on?" I asked. Gus and his wife owned a salon in San Antonio and the last we had spoken, they had just bought a fabulous new home.

Mama handed me a piece of paper, "Call your brother at this number when you get home tonight. It will be nice for him to speak to his sister."

As promised, I called Gus when I got back to the Poconos.

"What did mama and daddy tell you?" he asked.

"Daddy said, something about you 'not washing no hair,' and Mama just asked me to call you."

He exhaled, "I'm getting a divorce." He told me the longest story and all I could say was, "Wow." Gus was a real doer of the Word of God. He was totally against divorce but his wife committed adultery with one of their employees at the salon. He had moved out and was in truck-driving school in Dallas. I sat in a shocked silence and listened to his story for more than an hour. It felt good to be of support to another situation other than my own for a change.

"What about you?" he asked. I didn't really want to discuss it but Gus was my first-ever best friend so I told him the truth about Steven.

"I know everything already," he said, blowing me away. "Stevie called me at home in the middle of the night to ask me to come there to kill your husband for what he was doing to you."

See, my family is crazy, I thought.

Gus continued, "I spent two hours talking your brother down from killing him that night by telling him I'd come if he would wait for me to get there. I knew that he'd simmer down."

I started to cry because the impact of how this ordeal was affecting me, my family and friends, too, was just too much. I wasn't prepared to deal with any of it anyway, and now I had to help my family deal with something I wasn't sure how to navigate myself. It was only by the grace of God I was functioning at all. Steven's diagnosis had driven my brother to call Gus and ask for his help in killing him. I couldn't believe it. That's why my brother stayed around, he stayed to protect me. Between the Blood of Jesus and Stevie, all bases were covered.

We talked for three hours crying and praying, and reading Bible scriptures to one another for comfort. Gus had been nearby for every major event in my life, and while we had not spoken in a long time, I felt his genuine support and familiar comfort envelop me.

That Friday, I had a cold and was turning out the lights to go to bed when Missy started barking at the door. Steven had arrived in the truck with his sister.

"Look who's home, Missy," I said holding her collar to let them inside. I welcomed them both, helped to get Steven settled and offered food. Steven was dangerously thin, his face was a broken-out mess and he was walking shakily. The two of them barely looked my way or even said anything to me.

"I have a bad cold, so I was about to go to bed. Steven you sleep in our bedroom and I'll sleep in the guest room so you won't catch my germs."

"Where's my sister going to sleep if you sleep in the guest room?"

"Have you forgotten that there are two other rooms, an office with a futon and a pull-out couch in the TV room? She can sleep wherever she wants."

I knew what the deal was. He had decided to sneak up on me unannounced to see if I was going to be home with someone else or even home at all. Missy and I went to the guest room and I heard them watching TV most of the night.

Saturday morning arrived with my usual flurry of activities and I was out of the house by seven. Steven was always a late-riser, I could go to town, run several errands, get back home and cook breakfast all before he ever woke up.

I left Steven at home and went to work with food labeled in the fridge and medicines lined-up on the counter. When I got home that night the house was completely dark. I sat in the car a moment and prayed, "Lord, please don't let him be in this house dead. I have three requests: one, please don't let me come home and find him dead. Two, please don't let him die in this house. And three don't let me be there when he dies. Amen."

These were not unreasonable requests, but there are some things I'd rather not remember. I would hate to have to remember, this is the room I found him in, or watch someone take their last breath. Some people are OK with "being there" in the last moments. I felt that was a job for a professional. I was already wiped up emotionally, I didn't need anything else to rattle my fragility. I was sure God would honor the requests I had made in earnest and I went in the house.

Steven had slept all day without eating or drinking anything. He said he was very tired and cold. In spite of the traditionally warm weather, California was in the midst of a rainy cold-snap that lasted for the duration of his two month visit. He complained that he was freezing day in and day out while there. I gave him an herbal concoction laced with cayenne pepper to get his blood circulating. When I checked his extremities, sure enough he was blue.

I took him to emergency and he stayed in the hospital three days. The doctor just shook his head because he did not believe Steven was still alive.

"All indicators of his tests show that he should not still be here. Miss, on paper he's technically dead already," the doctor told me. It's just a matter of time. He has an iron-clad will. I've seen how he treats you and it seems as if he's hanging on just so he can punish you for some reason." That was an incredible revelation from a doctor. An outsider who only saw us once a month.

He's punishing me for being negative, I thought. I wrecked Steven's plan by not contracting AIDS and riding into the sunset to die with him, so he was trying his best to make me miserable while he waited to die.

CHAPTER SEVEN
The Preparation for Death

"When calamity comes, the wicked are brought down,
but even in death the righteous have a refuge."

Proverbs 14:32

When he came home from the hospital we made arrangements for me to leave the food in a cooler in the bedroom so he could easily get to his provisions.

My assistant rushed me out of a meeting to tell me Steven was on the phone with an emergency.

"Rabbit, I need you to come home," he said crying.

I braced myself, "What happened?"

"I went to the bathroom, and when I got off of the toilet I fell down. I couldn't get up off the floor so I had to drag myself to the bed and it took almost an hour to do it because I'm so weak. I need you to come home now, I need you!"

"I'm on the way." I opened the door to my vice president's office and simply said, "emergency," and she nodded.

On the bus home I put into action what I knew now needed to be done. Since I was working, Steven was clearly in no shape to be home alone all day. I thought of Ruthie. She and Clive had split-up and she was staying with a friend. She immediately said yes to my move-in offer.

When I relayed the details of Steven's episode to the doctor he told me the neuropathy (a loss of sensation in the extremities) was no longer a threat, but in full effect. That was the last day Steven walked.

A neighbor came in the next day every two hours to check on him until I could get home with the full-time help. Ruthie got settled into the guest room and was happy to be away from the city for a while and her situation. Her break-up was happening right under my nose and I never noticed the decline in their relationship. She and God let me know it was a good thing that I was so intensely taking care of my own house, I didn't notice what was happening anywhere else.

Steven loved Ruthie very much but he was displeased with the new arrangement. He reamed me for not taking a leave of absence in order to care for him myself. "And who is going to pay the mortgage and the electric heating bill if I take a leave?"

"You know you can ask your parents, they'll help you."

"Sure they will, but I'm not asking. My parents are retired, and they are enjoying themselves on the beaches of the world because they deserve it. I'm not loading anything extra on them. This is my cross to bear, the money can be easily made but I've got to go to work."

He made no bones in his displeasure of this arrangement It was a good thing that I loved working at Arista so much, because there was no way I could be in the house with Steven twenty-four-seven. Since the day he came home from California, I was sleeping in the guest room. He was so needy through the night, that I'd spend most of it running up and down the hall to comply with his requests. Finally, I made a soft pallet on the floor at the foot of the bed.

Steven literally woke me up every hour so that I could be of service to him. "I've got to use the bathroom," which usually meant using a urinal. He had been using a urinal for a long time and since urine is a body fluid – and the virus is transmitted through body fluids - it had to be handled like blood.

Miss Lucille had sent me a basket with assorted essentials to conduct at-home care. There were all sorts of cremes, sprays and ointments to prevent the skin from becoming dry and developing bed sores. The most important items were the latex gloves. Just like the hospital employees, I followed suit I took care of him with gloves.

He'd wake me, "I'm thirsty." I still maintained his well-stocked cooler next to the bed. He didn't need to ask me for anything cold to drink during the night.

"I want cinnamon toast." Steven consumed large quantities of cinnamon toast day and night alternately with cinnamon frosted Pop-Tarts, because I refused to let him eat that junk food ten times a day.

I knew that the virus loved and thrived in sugar, which is how he kept thrush in his mouth. Sweet things were all he wanted most times. The thrush is a condition that arises due to an over-run of yeast (candida) in the body and can at times manifest itself in the mouth. The yeast then settles in a moist, dark place and festers. If not properly controlled, too much candida would cause a person a systemic yeast problem which compounds any initial diagnosis. Ultimately, the culprit of such a yeast infection is sugar and the nasty whites – pasta, rice, white sugar, and flour.

Steven had a lifetime love affair with sweets. Claudette remembers that he had a bag of assorted candy the first day she met him in the 1980's. I did my best to educate him on the importance of nutrition in addition to medication. He would not listen. He also knew that he could manipulate Ruthie into giving him whatever he wanted to eat.

He would tell me, "I'm dying! Why do you care what I eat?! Why can't you just let me have some happiness. These are my last days and you're depriving me of the food I love. I hate you!"

I'd heard the "I hate you" lines spewed at me before, as well as at his sisters or about them. Steven was so angry at so many people, it was a shame to see my husband bitter. His already sour disposition festered into a toxic waste pool that he no longer concealed.

"You think just because Ruthie is here to help me that I'm letting you off the hook in taking care of me?" he would say as he woke me up every hour during the night. "There is no way you're getting a break. I'm going to make you do your wifely duties."

"Don't ever think you're making me do *any*thing," I would remind him calmly. "Now, what can I get you?"

The 90-minute bus ride to and from New York City was the only uninterrupted sleep I would get every day. Taking care of Steven was like having a newborn baby, but I had heard infants woke up every two hours. I was bordering on exhaustion. The bus sleep was the best ever and a couple of times I'd slept past my stop at Port Authority on 42nd Street and went to the end of the line at the World Trade Center. I would have to take the subway back to mid-town and I never minded because the sleep had been so good.

At work one day, the president of Black music called me into her office very formally. I grabbed a pad and ran down the hall to Jean's office. There sat the two vice presidents of Black music, Lionel and David, and Jean's assistant Michelle.

"Sit down," she ordered. The formality of it all had me thinking, I was fired. My heart was pounding.

Jean leaned over her desk and looked me square in the eye asking, "Why is it that we are just finding out you have a terminally ill husband at home, who is very close to death?"

I exhaled, *Oh, that*, I said to myself, knowing they had the stomach cancer story. "I'm sorry, I thought you all knew."

"No, we all just found out this morning," Jean said. "How come you didn't say anything?"

Lionel turned from the window, "No, what I want to know is, how is it that you are the brightest spot up in here and you're going through all this! I depend on seeing your smile every day!" he said pointing at me, complimenting my disposition and perplexed about my trouble all at the same time.

David interjected, "You keep us all smiling and upbeat no matter what and you've got this to deal with?"

Michelle, Jean's assistant, stood at the edge of the desk with her hand over her mouth in shock.

"You guys, this is no place for me to wear what's happening at home on my face. I've got a job to do..."

Lionel interrupted, "Which you do well."

"Thank you. I have to leave my house every day to have some sanity. I have full-time help and I don't start thinking about home again until I get off the bus and drive the 22 miles home. I basically start thinking about whether or not I will come inside and find him dead. I cannot carry a thought like that around with me all day. I thank you all for your concern but I'm God's girl for real, He's got me."

Jean confirmed, "Well, you're our girl too and it's killing us to hear you going through all of this. I don't know what to do for you to help. I'm going to give you a check for two hundred dollars. Can that help you?"

I started to get misty. "Yes, it will. Thank you so much," I said thinking of putting a dent into the phone bill.

"Good," she said writing a check. "And if you need some more, you better let me know."

I hugged them, excused myself and went to my desk to cry until I was interrupted by Ruthie calling, crying. Fortunately Arista had an 800 number so that call could be made without using George's card.

For Ruthie to call me at work crying while she was in my house caring for my dying husband was not a good sign. "What. Happened?"

"Girrrrrrl," she sniffled, "Steven has gone crazy."

"Yes, of course, he has dementia on top of a raging case of entitlement. A lethal combination."

"Joycie, as much as I'd like to stay, I can't. At first, I wasn't going to tell you. It's been going on for a week now, but he cussed me out until I cried today, telling me how fat I was and that he couldn't stand the sight of me. And to leave him alone, that you would do what needed to be done for him when he got home. And he sees now why Clive and I broke up. And how I would never find anyone to love me again the way he did because no one wants a fat wife."

"I'm so sorry, honey." All of these things Steven said to her were things that he knew would hit a nerve. Ruthie weighed about 300 pounds and I loved every ounce of her. She had a heart of gold that matched her lively personality.

I saw straight through Steven. He was trying to sabotage my efforts to provide care for him until I exhausted all of the possibilities and had to do it myself.

"I rebuke you in the name of Jesus," I said out loud. My assistant looked over at me and knew there was trouble. She was used to me praising Jesus aloud for anything by now.

Ruthie said, "I'm going to call Kim to get pick me up tonight, so you don't have to take me to the city." Even in her departure, and as bad as Steven had treated her, she thought of him first by making arrangements to be picked up from the Poconos.

I got right on the phone, made a master calendar, and put "Plan B" into action. First thing, get coverage for the next day. Pastor K.P. volunteered and made himself available every Wednesday. *Great -Wednesday's done*, I thought. Pastor K.P. had done us a huge favor by using one of our cars and taking over the payments. We had two cars and two trucks and it was very hard to juggle all of the finances. Pastor K.P. loved the Taurus station wagon and cared for it like it was his own.

By the time I got home that night, I had a calendar of care-givers, day-by-day. Then Steven got told off by me for hurting the feelings of my dear friend and I let him know of my displeasure.

I went over the new calendar and showed him I had booked care-givers two months out. Tyger would give up her vacation for a week along with cousin Mayla. Henzy from Indianapolis would be here ten days. My God sister Sloopy and dance buddy/cousin Pam would come for a few days, and of course the parents would come for a week. Stacey and Claudette were already coming every weekend, primarily for Stacey to put Steven into the sunk-in tub for a long soak.

There were none of Steven's family and friends who were available for this intensive duty of at-home care. His sisters did what I called drive-by visits on some weekends coming all the way to the Poconos from Long Island and returning in the same day. I did understand their plight, the oldest sister had two jobs as did the youngest, who was also caring for a toddler - - so she had *three* jobs. Plus, I don't care what went down in their lifetimes, in the last couple of years, or even yesterday, their brother was dying a slow and painful death. It was a hard reality to view, but the least they could have done was be more present.

He protested, "I don't know what's it gonna take for you to get a leave and come home to take care of me."

"Forget it," I said. Work, in all of its insanity, was a blip on the computer compared to Steven. It wasn't that I was trying to leave the work of caring for him to others while I did nothing, but my friends who knew, helped to rescue me. God had already saved me more than once, and my family and friends were saving me from the rest.

They all got an orientation about how to care for him and themselves.

Mayla and Tyger were an awesome combo. One had to have a strong stomach and physical strength to take care of a man bedbound. Mayla had to excuse herself when I showed them how to position Steven for bowel movements. He refused to wear diapers anymore, saying he didn't want the feces on himself. So, he'd lay on his right side and make the excrement onto a disposable bed lining. He then had to be wiped, apply the cream and seal it with the spray and carefully roll the waste and dispose of it.

Tyger would show up in the room with gloves and a mask because you never knew what the request would be when you were called. It was a good idea to do that and everyone started following suit. They made Steven eat, be nice and talk about all the things he was feeling but didn't think he could tell me.

After about three days, when I got home one evening they had an intervention with me. First, they were very complimentary about the job that I was doing and how Steven was, in spite of his condition, well-cared for and holding on.

"From now on, you must have at least two people here at all times," Tyger said emphatically.

Mayla agreed, "This is too much for any one person to handle. The cooking, running up and down the stairs, being careful all of the time. I don't know how you do it, LaJoyce."

"By the grace of God," I told them.

Tyger maintained her emphatic posture, "Either have two people here always, or it's time to get a nurse."

The next day I put into action getting a nurse through the insurance company. Sure enough, he was eligible for one. I was thankful for Tyger making the suggestion. My brain was so fried that sometimes I wasn't as on-the-ball as I needed to be. I tripled my health regimen since I wasn't getting enough sleep and made sure that I stayed away from any sugar which could weaken my immune health.

I was sad to see Tyger go, but she was a sweetie for giving up her vacation. As a flight attendant, the last thing I knew she wanted to do was get on a plane so she could serve someone hand and foot when that is what she did all day long.

She grabbed my face in her hands, "I'll be waiting for the day when you call me, and all I hear on the other end will be you crying. You won't have to say anything, you won't have to apologize. I'll know it's you and that day is coming." We cried our eyes out.

Mayla came every weekend after her one-week visit. I was worried about her doing all of that late night running up and down I-80 from New York to be with me, but she confessed, "I love you very much and I can't watch you going through all of this by yourself." Even though Mayla and I are cousins, we are more like sisters. She is actually my second cousin and my father Duke's first cousin. The age difference in she and my father and our spiritual walks forces us closer together.

It was great having so many come to help out, but my kitchen arrangement was in shambles. I couldn't find anything. While on a long boring conference call at work, I made labels for the cabinets to help keep everyone organized. That would end the care-givers calling me at work asking for things like the hot sauce.

The registered nurse Tracey came first thing every morning to check Steven's vitals. Tracey lives in our community just a little over a mile from our house. God sure worked that one out. The nurse's aids' schedules were for five hours a day. *Better than nothing*, I thought. This meant the friends could be present and not run around for five hours.

Henzy arrived for his week of service to find Steven not being able to keep anything down. He was throwing up constantly and the doctor feared that the sarcoma was spreading to his intestinal lining. The constant break-outs on his face were as a result of Karposi's sarcoma, a type of skin cancer that is a by-product for some people with AIDS. The sarcoma was ever-present and I continued to conduct the skin care regimen because he loved it. The truth was that he had begun to look like he had leprosy - not that any of us have ever seen a leper, but the Bible is descriptive enough to give our sanctified imaginations creative license to run wild.

Steven was scheduled for an immediate procedure by which a probe with a camera was inserted down his throat and the intestines were viewed on a screen. The doctor had stressed that if he found lesions as he suspected, he would probably die within a few days. I cried my eyes out at the hospital when the doctor made his announcement to us because I was worried about Steven's soul. He had not made any apologies directly to me for concealing the truth about his illness.

The only person I told about him harboring this secret was Henzy. He was my friend, but he has the compassion of Jesus on all matters. I knew I could trust Henzy to enter into prayer mode instead of running to find the nearest gun. He was and still is wired very differently than the typical man. Henzy truly exemplifies carrying the love of Jesus every day in every way.

Just as Steven was being rolled into the operating room, Henzy stopped them and prayed with Steven. "Is there anything you'd like to confess to the Lord right now?" he asked hoping for truth. "You know that there is nothing you can't tell God, if there is anything at all you'd like to make right with God or with anybody else, now is the time to make that confession."

His eyes bucked wide open, "There is nothing that I can think of I need to confess."

"Nothing? Henzy repeated trying to arrange his question another way. "Then is there anything you need to ask forgiveness of from your wife?"

"Other than I hope she is forgiven for not staying at home to take care of me, there's nothing." Henzy was troubled because it was clear Steven was lying.

"OK then, may God be with you," Henzy conceded. When Steven was rolled away, he took my hand, "You do know he's never gonna make that confession because he's so stubborn. You're going to have to tell other people about this, we can't let him die without confessing."

The doctor didn't find any lesions in his intestines but advised there was nothing more that could be done for him except to keep him comfortable. "I can recommend a hospice for him in Allentown," he said, giving me the number. "I understand from Steven you all have made arrangements for him to die at home." I didn't say anything but my eyebrow went up and the doctor knew that was a lie. He shook my hand saying, "Good luck."

Steven complained endlessly about the nurse's aid saying she made too much noise in the room while he was trying to sleep and that she was too rough. The agency was kind enough to assign another nurse. I then extended other parts of the house to the nurse outside of the bedroom, instructing them to enter when summoned or as needed so he wouldn't be interrupted. I wanted to cancel out any more of his complaining about things we could control.

There was nothing that could any longer control his fevers, shakes, vomiting, thrush, weak muscles, weight loss or foul disposition. AIDS was ravishing his body with a vengeance. I asked God, "Why do you keep taking him to death's door and saving him? Why are you allowing him to suffer so?"

God said plainly to me, *"I've got this, don't ask me again."* It seems as if I was witnessing on person's hell right here on earth. *Wow, vengeance really is the Lord's,* I thought.

My parents rolled in next by car. They proved to be an excellent tag-team. By now, everyone knew the truth and Mommie was furious. It was Henzy's strategy to tell others to increase the opportunity for Steven's confession. Maybe someone would be able to reach him for the sake of his soul. The opposite actually happened. It seems as if Steven knew we all knew the truth because of our constantly discussing the need to be free from anything that would keep him from entering the gates of heaven. He became even more cantankerous.

Steven went so far as to tell me, "I don't know what it is, but I no longer trust you." The magnitude of what he said kicked me in the face. He had a way of doing that. Saying things that were so hurtful it made you sit down. I had a seat on the side of the night stand and thought very carefully before I said anything.

My mind raced, *Don't Trust Me!* I screamed in my head. *I'm here still taking care of you and you don't trust me! Let's go back to the first hour we met and you lied to me about some bleeding ulcers. This whole marriage is based on a lie and I'm still here and you want to say you don't trust me.* I swirled the medicine in the cup I had brought to the room and contemplated giving him one too many of each, or not giving it to him at all. The medications were not helping him to get better because he was at death's door, but if given too much or not taken at all he'd probably die. I was contemplative about how he had come from the place of deep love for me to hate, and how I had come from deep love to the decision to take his life.

It was very clear to me - his actions all pointed to the fact that he considered me a non-entity, a vessel to be of service to him in the last days. A body to be a whipping post for him. He wasn't physically able to strike out but he did it every day with the one strong thing he had left, his tongue. And it had brought me to a place where his fate was absolutely in my hands.

"Yeah, you can't say anything to that," he picked at me for not responding to his statement of trust. He rambled something in the background but it faded to black as my thoughts of how to administer the medication bounced back-and-forth like a fierce tennis match in my head. I went back to what I know is unchangeable and unmovable and that is the Word of God. Whenever I get so angry that I see red, I seek His face right there. *"...well done, thou good and faithful servant; thou has been faithful over a few things, I will make thee ruler over many things; enter thou into the joy of the Lord."* (Mathew 25:21)

"Thank you Jesus," I said aloud and peace enveloped me.

"Yeah, He's the only one who can help you," Steven said dryly.

"He's the only one who can help you too, sweetie. I'm sorry you don't trust me anymore."

"Well, I don't!"

"Well, if I were you, I'd keep that feeling to myself. How you gonna say something like that to someone who brings you meals and your medicine? It really hurts me to know you don't trust me. Take this," I said handing him the medicine cup, "and re-think what you're saying to me." I saw him thinking as he tentatively reached for the cup. He knew what I was saying, but he didn't say he was sorry. His non-trust for me had settled deep in the bowels of his soul and it was by choice that he let it fester.

I knew that when Steven died, I had to still participate in the game of life. How I chose to play it, would depend largely on how I handled the task before me. If I took the high road, I knew there was a promise at the end of the rainbow made to me by God. If I took the low road, I was setting myself up for a miserable life. Bishop Eddie Long boomed in my memory, "If you don't exhibit faith, you will forever be seated in the misery."

Mommie only came to the bedroom to say good morning and good night. Instead of being phony, she chose kitchen duty churning out meals and keeping the dishes washed, which was a full-time responsibility for sure. Bo Daddy kept Steven company and did a lot of talking with him, hoping for some glimmer of remorse.

I got pulled out of a meeting at work for an emergency call from Mommie about Steven. "That boy done lost his mind! The nurse just came down here in tears saying that in all of her 15 years experience she has never been treated like Steven has treated her. And she has never been talked to the way he did to her," Mommie said out of breath and rushing her words together - - a sign she was maaad!

She continued, "That nurse left here crying just now and said she was not coming back." I looked at the clock, the nurse was only two hours into her shift. "What are you going to do?"

I exhaled, "I'm going to have to call hospice and see if there is a bed available."

"Good, that's what you better do, because he needs professional help. We've all tried to pitch in to help you, but he's just ridiculous. I don't care if he is sick. He just wants you to do it. Call hospice now!"

"I will, I will…" I answered reluctantly because I knew how Steven felt about the whole idea.

"I mean now!" she said flipping into Mommie the green-eyed monster who would snatch you through the phone.

"Right now," I conceded, because Mommie's wrath was worse than Steven's.

The sure sign that going to hospice was the right thing to do was that they just happened to get a room available that morning, the ambulance needed to transport just happened to have a cancellation that morning and a fanzine photo shoot with *Right On!* Magazine I had to do with Usher just happened to be re-scheduled. Photo shoots take all day, so there was nothing else on my calendar, making it easy to take off. God wiped out every excuse. He showed me that hospice was the right choice.

I didn't say a word to Steven about where he was going until the ambulance came. He cried like a baby and asked the ambulance attendants to pause in various parts of the house so that he could get one last look around.

"You do know I'm not coming back," he said to us all. "My wife here is sending me off to die in some strange place."

Mommie spoke up, "Haven't we all been here to help you?"

"Yes, I have to admit that, you've been here every step of the way making good meals and Bo keeping the jokes coming."

"Alright then," Mommie said, "It's just too much for LaJoyce to handle by herself. It's best that you get professional care now."

He wanted to pet the dogs right before leaving and asked that I get his pillow, his back rest, and some photos of his mom from the wedding to put in his room. He lingered in the foyer asking for this and that, stalling.

"I'm ready to leave now," he said to the attendants. "bye-bye house, I'll never see you again."

Bo and I trailed the ambulance an hour to Allentown. The hospice was a beautiful hospital. It almost looked too inviting, luxurious, warm and comfortable for both family and patient. If ever there was a way to die in a dignified manner, this was it.

Steven loved grandeur and was impressed with the place from the lobby to the elevator to his room. He was in rare form, cracking jokes, being the loveable Steven I fell head-over-heels for four years earlier. Bo kept nudging me because he was being so nice to everyone and it was a definite shift in his disposition.

"Rabbit, at least you did something right by picking a beautiful place where I'm going to die," he complemented.

We got his room all set up with photos and stayed the rest of the day. The doctors examined him and advised that if he lasted another seven days it would be a miracle. He was well under one hundred pounds, the sarcoma was all over his face and entire body, and he was consistently at a 101.4 temperature.

When we were leaving for the evening, I sat on the edge of the bed, sat him upright, and hugged him close. He told me off for bringing him to his final resting place but he knew it was best.

I phoned the family to let them know Steven was at hospice and probably had only seven days left and to make their way out to Allentown.

His little sister challenged my decision. "You know he wants to die at home," she lashed out at me.

"You know he's here acting a fool, sending 15-year veteran nurses screeching down the mountain, vowing never to return. He can't die here if there's no help," I stressed. "The at-home program worked until he ran off all of the professional help. Here are the directions to the hospice." Those girls who showed up every once in a while were NOT going to worry me.

Bo Daddy stripped the bed sheets, comforters and plastic mattress cover and washed down the mattress with bleach, turned on the ceiling fan, and opened the windows wide. Then he mopped the carpet with a bleach water solution, while I lit scented candles. "I want to see you off of this floor and sleeping in your own bed tonight, you hear me," he scolded as he continued to disinfect.

The room never did have a sick-room feel or smell, but you knew it was. When Bo Daddy got finished, the room was light and airy, the heaviness was gone. I too felt lighter because I knew Steven was getting care that I could not possibly give him.

My parents left a day early and I made preparations to receive my girls from Chicago, Pam and Sloopy. We were more like family than friends which is why they were up for duty next. Since my schedule was air-tight, there were no days uncovered. They still wanted to come even though Steven was in hospice. They'd take care of me, they said.

I scooped them off of the plane in Allentown for their four-day stay and we went to visit Steven. Sloopy busted into the room with her cheery manner and she brought him a barrel of laughs. Pam excused herself after five minutes. When she didn't come back in half an hour, I found her in the visitor's lounge crying her eyes out.

Her father had recently died of cancer and I hadn't been able to be there for her. "I thought I had more time with him," she cried about her father. "I can't do this. I thought I was stronger, but it's bringing up too much emotion."

I hadn't had a chance to properly grieve her father either and my tears matched hers. "You know how I loved him. He taught me how to mix and blend medicinal teas." Her father was the first person who lived the organic lifestyle I had come to embrace also. He always had some tea on their stove and in the fridge, one that usually tasted really bad, but was really good for you. He was so happy when I went to work at GNC in high school and he encouraged me to learn as much as I could during my employment.

Pam sat in the lounge for hours crying because she didn't want to face Steven in his condition. The reality of what I was dealing with didn't help her emotionally and I had to leave her alone crying because it was not a time for me to fall apart. The nurses were prepping me for every stage of the slow death because Steven was standing at the door. The booklet written by the family of Karen Ann

Quinlin was an incredibly helpful tool in recognizing the end-stages of one who is dying.

It is never easy in making arrangements for the one you love to die. Even when you know the day is coming, it is a laborious undertaking to pick up that phone and call the undertaker. I did so at the urging of the nurses who were asking who would handle the body. Steven wanted to be cremated. I wanted to comply with his wish but I did not agree with cremation.

Steven told me he didn't want me to come over the weekend because his sisters were coming and he wanted to visit with them alone. I had made an agreement with myself to say yes to whatever Steven wanted. With only days to live, he was running the show.

Hospice nurses are pure angels, not only do they care for the dying patient but they care for the family. They walked me through everything. Before leaving every day, they told me what to expect the next, and they'd be right.

Pam, Sloopy and I had a pajama huddle every night during their visit. Pam was the chef and Sloopy provided much needed comic relief. They fed me fantastic meals and food for my soul. They scratched my dandruff, washed my hair, gave me a facial, manicure, pedicure and talked about me - as only your good girlfriends can - for letting myself fall apart. And just like a mother caring for a sick child, they tucked me into bed at a decent hour for a good night's sleep.

I felt re-fueled and re-charged by the time I dropped them at the Allentown airport at 5 a.m. and I swung by the hospice before heading to the city to work to check on Steven. He wasn't speaking any longer. He was really glassy-eyed and making motions with his hands. The doctor said that his vocal cords had been arrested by lesions from the sarcoma. He was being fed intravenously and the nurses said he would probably die within the next 48 hours.

I scooped-up Steven real close and held him for a long time. I told him I loved him and that I would be back that evening. He grunted and stroked my hair. I laid him back down and we did our pointer high-five before leaving.

I ran out of that place thinking *hold on Steven, because Mommie and Bo Daddy are back in two days.* I sped 40 minutes from Allentown back to the Poconos just in time to board the bus to the city. When Tyger came she supplied me with a bag-full of sermons from her brother-in-law Bishop Trotter. It seemed to me that Bishop was ministering directly to me. There was one tape called "Lord, I Need a Jump!" He made the correlation between needing a jump in a car to needing a jump from Jesus. I would have my arm all out of the window praising on that one! It was my favorite.

I had accomplished a major coup at work by garnering the cover of *Vibe* Magazine for The Notorious B.I.G. AKA Biggie, AKA Biggie Smalls and his wife Faith Evans. The shoot was on the waterfront underneath the Brooklyn Bridge. *Vibe* chose a vintage black convertible in which Faith and Biggie were dressed like a gangster and his girl sitting in the back seat.

It was a 90-plus degree July day in the city and there was not an ounce of cool relief for us exposed to the sunshine doing that photo shoot, not even next to the water.

There was a lot of running around to do for that particular shoot, so I had reserved a car for the day. My favorite drivers, brothers Nir and Jay, lived just across the water near me in New Jersey and I always requested them when going home late nights or for early morning pick-ups. I checked-in with the hospital and the nurse told me that Steven was definitely going to make his transition soon.

"When are you coming?" she asked, concerned that I wasn't there already. I knew I had asked God for me not to be there when it happened and I knew my request would be granted.

"I'll be there this evening after work," I assured her. "Feel free to call me on the following number to keep me posted," as I gave her the number for Nir's car phone. In 1995, we weren't surgically attached to a cell phone. Back then, they were very expensive and car phones were more accessible and affordable.

The photo shoot was sailing smoothly, while Faith and Biggie were eating up the opportunity to finally show the industry they were a bona-fide couple who had weathered a stormy marriage. Meanwhile, the nurse was calling me every hour with an update.

"His breathing is shallow. What time will you be here?" she asked.

I answered, "After work this evening."

"His pupils are dilating. What time will you be here?"

"After work."

"He's starting to lose his grip. What time will you be here?"

"After work."

Her calls went on like this all day long. I felt as if I was there with those up-to-the-minute reports of his demise. Like the kids say these days, that's just too much information. I couldn't deal anymore. I thanked God I was not in the office trying to handle the reality of my husband's last day alive. A photo shoot was fast-paced action that required my attention and I was thankful for just the right diversion.

During our lunch break at around three, Biggie took me to the side.

"How you doin'?" he quizzed me genuinely concerned.

I furrowed my eyebrows because I'd never seen him so tender. "I'm good."

"No you not. I know what's going on with you. I see you been cryin'. I see you runnin' back-and-forth to the phone in the car. How's your husband?"

I could only shake my head and a tear popped out. He scooped me up in a bear hug and rocked me, "Listen, go home and take care of your business. This is almost over here."

"No, it's only half over, I have to make sure…"

"I promise I won't embarrass you," he smiled, cutting me off and knowing why I was monitoring his every move. Biggie had a history of going off at photo shoots, screaming out that he wouldn't do this or that and then summoning me to put out the fires.

"I worked hard to get this cover, Biggie, you better not embarrass me or you'll never have another one." Ah, the power of a publicist, whatever you can do, you can un-do.

"I won't cuz I wants me another cover, but you go on to the hospital," and he kissed me on top of my forehead and turned me toward the car with a little shove. I didn't even look back. It wouldn't have mattered because I couldn't see a thing for the tears.

Nir wasn't ready to get off for the day so he drop-switched me with his brother Jay, and I advised the hospital that I was on my way. The nurse sighed relief but I was a nervous wreck inside praying for peace to calm my chattering teeth.

God, in all of His honoring of my prayer, created the most monstrous traffic jam and it took us more than three hours to make the 90- minute trek to the Poconos. I had decided to spend the night at the hospital but I didn't have any clothes and I hadn't made arrangements for the dogs to be fed so I went home first. I had another huge photo shoot with Deborah Cox the next day, so I needed clothes.

Driving to Allentown I ran into crawling traffic. The radio said there was an over-turned tractor trailer in the direction I was headed. I ducked off at the next exit and took the back roads that I had heard of but had never traveled all the way to Allentown to avoid the traffic.

I was singing, *"We have come this far by faith, and we are leaning, leaning on the Lord. We are trusting, trusting in his Holy Word. Cause He's never failed me yet..."* When the elevator doors opened, the nurse was standing there. She looked at the clock, which read 10:22 and she looked at me carrying my clothes asking, "Didn't you speak to the doctor?"

"No, I've been caught up in traffic everywhere for the last five hours."

"Well, he called you to let you know that Steven died at 9:05."

"He did?" I asked unbelievably.

You know it's going to happen. You're told it will happen, but when it does, it's like a karate kick to your stomach by a black belt who's really angry with you.

She helped me off of the elevator and took my overnight bag, "He wasn't alone, I was with him," she assured me.

"You were? Thank you," I managed to say. I was shocked because God had definitely orchestrated the day. Created traffic like none I'd ever seen. Causing a diversion at work and honoring my prayer, *please don't let me be there when he dies.* "May I use the phone?" I asked.

She seated me at the nurses station. "Wouldn't you like to go in to spend some time with him before you start making calls?"

"No."

She knelt in front of me. "You should go in so that you will have closure."

"No."

"If you don't go you may regret never having said good-bye."

"Miss, I have been saying good-byes for the last two years. We had our good-bye's again this morning. I choose to remember him like I saw him last. I don't want to see him dead. I don't want that memory."

Another nurse abruptly picked up the phone to call the Chaplain. In seconds a rotund man was kneeling before me trying to convince me to go in that room.

"All of you hear me," I said. "Thank you for everything you have done for us both. You are God's angels for sure. But nothing can make me go into that room. I am at peace with my soul in not seeing him dead."

They all stared at each other. I heard another nurse in the background say to someone else, "She's traumatized."

I snapped my head in her direction, "No, I'm not traumatized. This is an example of how you stand up when you have the peace and the love of Jesus to hold you up. Father, will you pray with me?"

He was now smiling, he understood what I was saying, "Yes, child." He prayed a beautiful prayer and my tears flowed freely. "Amen."

"May I have Steven's glasses, photos, wallet and watch from the room please?" I asked the nurse.

"What about everything else?" she asked.

"If you could throw it away, I'd appreciate it." The priest was holding my hand.

"Thank you Father, I'll be fine."

"Is there anyone at home?" he asked. Wow, there was no one at home. Isn't that just like God to fix it so there is no one else around but Him to lean on in your darkest hour?

I shook my head no and asked, "Is it OK if I make several phone calls?" The nurse pushed a phone in my direction. First call was to Steven's sisters who said they'd meet me at home. Mommie and Bo Daddy said they'd leave first thing in the morning. My senior publicity director at work Jackie advised me to handle my business at home and she'd handle my work responsibilities.

The nurse brought the things I requested from Steven's room and she made one last attempt to get me to see him. After refusing by thanking each of them for their compassion and care, I left exactly the way I came that evening - - singing... *We have come this far by faith, and we are leaning, leaning on the Lord. We are trusting, trusting in His Holy Word. Cause He's never failed me yet..."* That was July 19, 1995.

CHAPTER EIGHT
The Laying to Rest

"Come unto me, all ye that labour and are heavy laden and I will give you rest. Take my yoke upon you, and learn of me; For I am meek and lowly in heart: and ye shall find rest unto your souls for my yoke is easy and my burden is light.
Matthew 11:28-30

I got in my car after learning my husband had died after a two-year battle with AIDS and it was an eerie feeling to know that he was gone - for real, forever. I was drained physically as if someone had literally sucked the life out of me. As soon as I started the car my tape blared, "Lord, I Need a Jump!" Did I ever! I contacted my neighbors the Parkins family and had them to get their two kids, whom I called my two sons, ready so they could enter the house with me. I had a funny feeling about going into the house by myself the first time.

Jelani set up a video and walked the dogs, while Gyasi helped me in the bedroom to toss out all of the sick-care items immediately. I went on a cleaning frenzy. By the time we were finished, it looked like a sick person had never been in the house. I guess it was just busy-work, but I needed to stay busy until his sisters arrived.

The next day, we went to the mortician's office to finalize the cremation and no one made a move to pay for the expense but me. It was settled that they would keep his ashes next to Mama Mo's at their house.

For the funeral we all decided to wear white. George was on the program to play but his mother suffered a stroke the morning of the funeral and he couldn't come.

Steven had made special requests for singers and speakers at his service and everyone complied.

Bishop Sam spoke, "I remember when LaJoyce met Steven. EVERYthing was, Steve said, Steven bought, Steve gave! Steve, Steve, Steve!" he said mimicking me in my voice. Everyone roared with laughter.

My friend Arlene sang his favorite song by BeBe and CeCe Winans, "Don't Cry For Me" a cappella and there wasn't a dry eye in the place.

Pastor K.P. told the truth about Steven being grumpy on the days he cared for him. "We had good times and not so good times," he said honestly.

The eulogy was delivered by a new pastor at Steven's home Lutheran Church so it was important that those who knew him spoke to paint a real picture of the Steven we all knew.

After the service I was relieved not to attend a burial. We had the repast at his sister's house and it was there that I buried Steven and the last bit of a relationship I had with them. Leaving his ashes there was just like putting him in the ground to me. I knew that if I did not maintain a relationship with his sisters, then we wouldn't have one. I had done enough, and my vow was to Steven, not to his sisters.

The relationship from their family I chose to maintain was that with Uncle Charles, Aunt Peggy and their kids Kathy, Fabia and Charles Jr. To this day we still call one another family. When I hugged his sisters goodbye, I knew that would be the last time I'd see them. My goodbye was sincere, firm and final.

I had taken a week off of work to handle the aftermath of laying my husband to rest. Bright and early Monday morning I dressed, ready to handle business in town.

Mommie saw me walking out the door. "Where are you going this time of morning?"

"I'll be back this evening." With a briefcase full of death certificates and all of the pertinent papers to run my life and my household, I went all over town and when I returned I was once again legally LaJoyce Celeste Hunter on everything.

I threw my driver's license on the table for display and announced that I was back!

Bo Daddy had only one concern, "What you going to do with all this house?"

"I plan to live in it. Steven had better credit with all those credit cards and even though I had no credit history, I had the cash. This here is MY house," I reminded him.

I spent a lot of time that week sleeping, especially after Mommie and Bo Daddy left. I knew that was a sign of grieving. In the middle of my grieving period, Steven's oldest sister called to ask that I sign-off of a property in Queens via quick claim deed.

"Why do you need my signature at all?" I asked.

"Well, when Steven was in the hospital last time we FedExed the papers to him so they could be signed and notarized. So, now all you have to do is sign the deed because the notary stamped it but forgot to sign it, so it is not valid."

Her call was the first I had heard of all this, "Oh really. Well that's what you all get for sneaking. It seems that you all are just busy sneaking and lying all the time. If you would have asked me in the first place to get it done, it would have been done right. Since you didn't, I'm not signing anything." And that, was the last time we spoke on the phone.

I found a grief counseling group through Catholic Services that met once weekly. After the first meeting, I understood how important it was to let go of things that I was holding on to, like clothes and photos. That made so much sense to me - clean out the closet. I called Stacey, Uncle Charles and Charles, Jr. over to have their pick before it all went to the community outreach center.

I sat on the floor in a corner and cried as they picked out and tried on the very expensive clothes that once brought Steven so much joy. Claudette acknowledged how hard it was for me to be able to get rid of such personal items. I needed them all gone. It was a cleansing and a purging that was necessary to move forward from my place of pain. I had to regain my personal power - - and fast. The only way to do that was to rest in Jesus.

It took me a while to sort through the photos of us all over the house. I knew definitely that those had to go. No way did I want photos of my dead husband staring at me from anywhere. I made separate pouch packs for all family members and Godmother Martha too. They included photos from the wedding until the last time we ever took pictures.

At work, I knocked on Jackie's door. "Have you got a minute? I want you to see something." I pulled out all of the photos and she smiled at them. Jackie was one of the industryites Steven had snuggled up to and loved dearly. The feeling was mutual with all of us. I have known her since the 1980's upon my early arrival to New York City and she was always like a big sister to me. She had called me to come get the job at Arista for which she had referred me. It was during that moment of reminiscence that I got the courage to tell her the truth about Steven's illness. She burst into tears and pushed the photos to the floor.

I went around to her side of the desk to comfort her. Jackie is not the crying type but this hurt her deeply. "I promise you, I'm OK. I promise you I'm negative."

I knew this was a story I was going to have to tell over and over again, but it was necessary for MY healing. I understood his sister's position in maintaining his privacy while he was alive, but it made not an ounce of sense to me to continue to keep the privacy of a dead man. I sort of went on a crusade after that. Calling people who had been incredibly supportive of me and making lunch, dinner and weekend dates with them to find the right time to tell them the truth. The news rocked every single person in the same manner.

I even tried to dig-up the women with whom he told me he had been intimate. I was only able to track down one of them through his neighbor, but she denied having sexual relations with him. *Hmmm, even after his death, I'm still uncovering the truth,* I thought. The woman was thankful I had called at all.

Everyone wanted to basically know the same thing, how did I keep it together? My answer is, only by the grace of God. See, that's when you know it's God because when you should be out of your mind, you're not out of your mind. I had a resolve because in my heart Steven was fully forgiven. What he did was all so pedestrian, common, dirty and cruel - - mostly just cruel.

It really is criminal to intentionally do harm. In order for him to do that I had to be considered a non-entity by him. He made a conscious effort to be passive aggressive and it is this behavior that allows HIV/AIDS to proliferate. It is the main reason why the numbers of infections are staggering today.

I was spared by the Blood of Jesus to not become a statistic. What I endured was to fulfill what God planted inside of me that has to do with the salvation of the world. The faith that I carry is because the Bible says, *"to each one, God has given a measure of faith."* I have learned to be faithful to what God said in the little stuff, because it is not faith for the stuff, but faith for the journey. Ultimately, it is faith that excites God.

This journey did not rob me of my faith, but definitely put it under fire.

CHAPTER NINE
The Restoration of Love

"A new commandment I give unto you, that you love one another; as I have loved you, that ye also love one another. By this shall all men know that you are my disciples, if you have love one to another."
John 13:34-35

Mommie was really worried about my socialization after many months. She would ask me every Friday with expectation, "What are you doing this weekend?"

"Not a thing," was my standard reply. I was running around like a crazy woman all around the country with Arista artists and attending various functions through the week. I needed the weekend to replenish and it had not a thing to do with Steven. Mommie wasn't buying that a bit.

I asked God to help make me ready for the man of God that He wanted me to have. I understood very clearly that I also had to take responsibility for my actions in the Steven debacle. Because the Bible is very clear in Proverbs 18:22: *"He who finds a good wife finds a good thing."* It does not say, *she* who finds a good *husband*. Yes, when we met there were fireworks between us, but I didn't have to place my stake in him and make the declaration to all of my friends – "that's gonna be my husband!" I then proceeded to whip it on him good, by adding log after log onto the fireworks to garner a marriage proposal.

Once the wedding date was locked, I did a lot of being consumed by the planning of *my* wedding. God was putting things right in front of me in plain view, that if I was not so busy planning a wedding, maybe I would have seen some of the signs. But at age 28, when all of your friends have already walked down the aisle and you've got the closet full of bridesmaids dresses, you look the other way at a lot of things. Don't do it! When someone shows you who they are, believe them.

Back in 1990 a girl didn't need to ask questions such as, have you ever had a homosexual experience? Or, have you taken the AIDS test? And, what's your status? While I don't have concrete proof - like catching Steven in the bed with another man - I have a compilation of lies that spiral in that very direction. Disappearances with his pals from out-of-town, disappearances and weak excuses about his whereabouts at odd times, his severe homophobia, and of course his status of having full-blown AIDS as if it showed up one day like the common cold. HIV is not some disease that sneaks up on you. Steven was in denial to the nth degree and last I checked, The Nile is a river in Egypt. It is time that denial let our people go.

Bottom line with my responsibility in this, is that I didn't ask enough questions. I wasn't educated enough to get *myself* tested, and I didn't seek God. Matthew 6:33 in the Bible says, *"But seek ye first the kingdom of God and His righteousness and all things shall be added unto you."*

But in the words of the dearly departed Biggie, *"If you don't know, now you know."* I only share my story so you know what to look out for, don't make it *your* story and risk becoming a statistic. Now YOU know.

As bad as things had gotten I knew God was still God. You cannot conquer what you do not confront. I also knew I could not just sweep it under the Cross. I serve the one true master who helped me to overcome all, but I first had to face Him. It made no sense to me to murmur and complain, because the test was not to see what I was going to do. God already knew what I would do. But God's grace is the test to show us where we are.

Some people have gone so far as to say that Jesus had forsaken me – maybe for a moment in my disobedience He had. Delayed obedience is disobedience. During my wilderness experience, God was arranging some things. Only when He was ready did He bring me back onto the scene with a fresh anointing that cannot be denied if, this time, I did what He has ordained. Before an anointing there is always a crushing, and after a breaking there is always a blessing...

Christmas 1995 – I arrived in Chicago with an air-tight calendar that I intended to follow. I had arranged with Gus to visit after Mommie, Sloopy and a group of us girls went to see *Waiting To Exhale*. When I arrived at the Brookshire house, I found Gus had waited for me all day because he didn't know what time I'd arrive. Mama Brookshire had a fabulous meal on the stove and I sopped up string bean juice with my corn bread, while Tony, Gus' teenaged son, serenaded us, trying to convince me that he was the next Usher. It was good to be home in the place of my familiar.

Gus came home with me and he helped me do all of the cake and pie baking. We had so much catching up to do. We had not had a marathon conversation since the spring when he was in truck driving school, so we were overdue. His divorce was final July 15th. We were amazed that our marital situations were both concluded during the same week.

"You've hugged everyone today except me," Gus pointed out. "Come give me a hug." Gus was the best hugger in the world. It took only five minutes for us to be fully in-love again, and before he left we were kissing on the steps just like when I was 16, with him standing one step below me so we could be eye-to-eye. It was a magical moment, like taking a powerful youth pill.

I went to Liberty Temple with Darlyn, my best-friend from Jr. High School. Apostle Clifford Turner was totally awesome. She and I kept nudging each other as his message was for us both.

"I need you to drop me off," I told her.

Recognizing the house Darlyn said, "If you and Gus get back together, I'm going to believe in Fairy Tales!"

With a giggle I said, "Believe it baby!" and I kissed her Merry Christmas. She was so happy I could hear her praising right there in the car.

Gus and I attended a midnight Christmas Eve service at St. Albie's, a church in our neighborhood that used to have dances every Saturday night when we were teens – dances that I could never attend, by the way. Gus would go and call me from the phone booth and talk to me for the duration of the dance. Before the service, he took me to the phone booth he used to call me from and showed me where he had carved out Gus + LaJoyce way up high.

A friend of mine asked me did I ever think that God would hook me up with the man of my past, to be the man of my future and my present? I had to think about those questions and honestly say no. I promised God that the next time, I'd follow His leading. LaJoyce's leading was ALL wrong! I did ask that whomever he sent, be a man of valor and one who could be the Bishop of our household. I also needed the man to have an understanding of me. With all I'd experienced we would have to connect spirit-to-spirit, because I had become an extremely complex individual.

Gus was definitely like-minded and like-spirited. He followed the Bible in all matters. At six-feet-four, he was as rock solid in his faith as he was in his stature. He too had a serious wound that would take time to heal from his marriage. Together, as boyfriend and girlfriend we would heal together by seeking and serving the Lord.

We did a lot of visiting between Chicago and the Poconos during 1996. He asked for my hand in marriage in a tuxedo shirt and bow-tie, and presented me with a whopper pear-shaped diamond ring on bended knee.

Our ivory wedding invitation embossed in gold, with a boy angel kissing a girl angel read:

The Beginning of a Harmonious Life
will commence on
Saturday, April twenty-sixth
nineteen hundred and ninety-seven
As I will finally marry my childhood sweetheart
my Soul Mate in Christ
and my first best friend.
Come rejoice and witness the wedding of
LaJoyce Celeste Hunter
and
Gus William Brookshire, Jr.
One o'clock in the afternoon
Reaching Out For Jesus Christian Center
Stroudsburg, Pennsylvania

We had 200 guests from everywhere celebrate our special day. Bishop Sam married us and Pastor K.P. conducted the ceremony where we married Gus' son Tony into the union. We sealed the service with Holy Communion and we were pronounced man and wife! There are people from our childhood who still can't believe that Gus and I are really married...finally.

We did not have the issue of the name change because I had been writing LaJoyce Brookshire since I was 12 years old. Gus gave me diaries every year from 1976 to 1981 for Christmas. I'm convinced that is where my story-telling of daily events truly developed. In the back of those diaries, I have written the names of the six children we wanted to have and of course LaJoyce Celeste Brookshire written in script, print, bold-face with a marker, and with crayon!

I reclaimed the love of my life by keeping Jesus pre-eminent in mine. Where Christ is in the center, he holds all things together, as it says in Colossians.

While Gus and I don't have the six kids we dreamed of in our teenage years – because we wised up - we are blessed with one amazing little girl, Brooke Angel, who lights up any room she enters.

The Lord made it possible for me to trust and love again because I trusted wholly in Him. *"He brought me forth also into a large place; He delivered me because he delighted in me. The Lord rewarded me according to my righteousness, according to the cleanness of my hands in his eyesight. ...As for God, his way is perfect..."* Psalms 18:24-25.

God indeed is perfect. I trusted Him when I was at a terrible crossroad, and when I took the time to listen to HIM, he said, *"I'll bless you."* I'm living that blessing each day with a husband who loves the Lord, and a daughter, too. I am additionally blessed to be negative and still be in the game of life. And I am for certain, that the only way to play it is with God before you.

Our mission statement in the Brookshire home is:

"Every day in every way, present God's Word as a dying man to dying men, as we seek the Kingdom of God first because ALL things, not just some, but ALL things will be added unto us."

When you seek God, many truths will uncover themselves. When you seek God, you may not be inclined to harbor a horrible secret of your son, your brother, your friend, or your spouse. When you seek God, only the truth will make you free. When you seek God, you will know that secrets are just lies not spoken, that can kill and destroy like the enemy who walks the earth seeking whom he can devour.

My final thought is one from Bishop Sam, with a little addendum from me - - *"Wherever you go, whatever you do, and whomever you do it with, if God doesn't give it to you, it's not worth having."*

And if I had to say Amen, I think I'd put one right there.

CHAPTER TEN

The Resources

"My people are destroyed for lack of knowledge."
Hosea 4:6

Here are the most recent devastating statistics on HIV/AIDS according to the National Centers for Disease Control & Prevention (CDC) and the Henry J. Kaiser Family Foundation:

As of 2003:
-African Americans account for 51% of all HIV infections in the 32 states that require reporting

-African American women account for 69% of HIV diagnosis among females from 2000-2003

-In African American females infected, 80% were attributed to heterosexual transmission of which only 17% are due to intravenous drug use

-In 2003 Black Women accounted for 67% of HIV/AIDS cases
Latinas 16%
White women 15%

-In 2002, AIDS was among the leading cause of death for women overall and was the number one cause of death in Black women between 25-34, their child bearing years

-Since beginning of epidemic Blacks have accounted for 37% of all persons with AIDS

-By December 2003 nearly 196,000 Blacks were estimated to have died from AIDS - - 9,048 of them occurred in 2003 alone.

-African American teens aged 13-19 represent 15% of all cases however, accounted for 65% for new AIDS cases reported for teens in 2002.

-A similar impact can be seen for African American children under age 13 most likely perinatal transmission, but can also be sex.

-Estimated AIDS prevalence among African Americans increased by 37% between 1999 and 2003, compared to a 22% increase among whites.

HOW TO STAY WELL

In addition to being covered by the Blood of Jesus in not becoming infected with the virus after multiple exposures, I am convinced it is due to the holistic lifestyle that I have practiced since my late-teens. As a result, my immune system is rock-solid. Now as Dr. LaJoyce Brookshire, Naturopathic Doctor, Master Herbalist, and Minister of Health, I'd like to share some ways that you too can bolster your immune health.

–Drink half your body weight in ounces of high-quality filtered or spring water daily (i.e. if you weigh 150 pounds, then you should drink 75 ounces). Remember, if you feel thirsty, then dehydration has already set-in.

Water has been my primary beverage for more than 20 years. I always add lemon to my water in restaurants, because lemon kills any bacteria that may be in the water by making the water acidic, while becoming alkaline ash in the stomach. I also like to cut-up fresh fruit filling the bottom of a pitcher with berries, watermelon or kiwi and pouring water over the fruit. I let the container sit in the refrigerator over night and in the morning I have real fruit water. Nothing added and the water totally takes on the flavor of the fruit.

Additionally, I drink most of my water laced with chlorophyll because it mimics red blood cells and aids to strengthen them. I like the brand by Nature's Sunshine which has a flavor of spearmint and makes it more palatable as a primary beverage. I pour in the chlorophyll concentrate until the water becomes dark green. Yes, I carry bottles of green water - - it's a great conversation piece.

A must read:

Your Body's Many Cries for Water: You're Not Sick, You're Thirsty

by Dr. F. Batmanghelidj

-Make a Super Food green drink daily loaded with chlorophyll, spirulina, wheatgrass, barley, blue-green algae. I recommend Kyo-Green and I put it in a smoothie with frozen fruit and Green Goodness juice by Bolthouse Farms. I also recommend SuperGreens loaded with 67 grasses and leaves to restore alkalinity to the body. Get at www.innerlightfoundation.org.

A must read: *The Ph Miracle* by Dr. Robert O. Young

-Take a liquid multi-vitamin daily. I am an advocate of liquids and powders versus pills, because they are bio-available for immediate use in the body. I recommend E3Live, the world's first and only fresh-frozen live Aphanizomenon flos-aquae (AFA). It contains more chlorophyll than wheatgrass, 60% high quality protein, all B Vitamins including B12, Omega-3 & Omega-6, digestive enzymes and anti-aging nutrients. It comes frozen to your door by FedEx.

Try it for yourself – 888.800.7070 or www.e3live.com

(referred by Dr. Brookshire.)

-The More White Bread, The Sooner You're Dead!

Eliminate the white's – bread, pasta, bread, rice and sugar. These are devitalized foods that tear down your immune system. Never eat white bread, choose multi-grain breads instead. Never use margarine or butter spreads, choose REAL butter always. Do not consume ANY aspartame products – Equal, Sweet 'n' Low, Splenda, these are all poison's and the primary culprit for new diseases with fancy names like Fibromyalgia.

A must read: *Back To Eden* by Jethro Kloss

A must subscribe: www.mercola.com

-Eat mainly green, leafy, and raw vegetables. Your diet should consist of 60 percent raw foods. To accomplish this, I begin with a full plate of salad as if it were going to be my meal, then I put my hot food on top of the salad. I get the hot/cold and crunchy/soft combo – which I love – with every bite. Remember, my nickname was Rabbit...

This will also help you to accomplish alkalinity in the body. Acid in the body is the introduction of ALL disease. Buy saliva Ph Strips in the health food store to test yourself regularly.

A must read: *Alkalize or Die* by Theodore A. Baroody

-Eat at least 5 fruits a day. I eat my fruits for breakfast and this way I know I have eaten them all. Be careful not to combine fruits with other foods, as they putrefy in the stomach making digestion impossible. Fruits should be eaten alone, at least two hours after eating, or before eating. Do not combine melons with other fruits, eat them alone.

I like to cut my fruits and freeze them so that they are readily available for making a smoothie instead of using ice. Or, I love to puree fruits and use them as ice cubes in homemade lemonade, juices or champagne.

A must read: *Fit for Life* by Harvey and Marilyn Diamond

A must subscribe: www.notmilk.com

-Eliminate beef and pork from the diet. These foods take too long to digest and makes your elimination system work over-time. You will lose that 'sluggish' feeling after eating if you eliminate these foods.

-Buy organic or local farm fresh foods as a rule. Yes, organic foods are more expensive but I say, you can pay now or pay later. The old adage: You Are What You Eat - is true. You are not only what you eat, but also what you digest, and what you eliminate. You should have an elimination after every meal for optimum colon health. Death really does begin in the colon. To aid in digestion, try digestive enzymes before each meal.

-Go to bed! I have been a sleepy-head since I could remember, but I rise very early. I've learned that this is the pattern of our body clocks being at one with nature. We are designed to rise and retire with the sun. The <u>only</u> time your body can repair itself is when you are sleeping. Make a point of retiring at night by creating a ritual for yourself. I like to bathe, relax by reading, journaling, or changing channels, turn-off the lights, the TV and sleep. My internal clock awakens me during the 4 o'clock hour. When I wake-up, I get up.

-Get exercise. I like to power walk and attend dance classes. When I can't get outside, as I run errands I park in the furthest corner of the parking lot and walk. I take stairs whenever I can and clean my own house.

-Eliminate stress. Examine your life and take a look at the things that may stress you. In many cases it may be your job, but if you have a "Plan B" it will be easier to say 'good morning' at the 9-5.

If it is a toxic relationship, seek counseling with that person. If the person means you well, they will honor your request. Upon such a suggestion, you will uncover the truth. I like to take my stresses to the bathtub and as I wash away the day, I consider all that has troubled me. When I release the drain, as an exercise of my faith, I allow all I washed off to leave me, by going down the drain.

For those stresses that sneak up on me when I'm not near my tub, I keep a bottle of the holistic product **Bach Flower Rescue Remedy** in my purse and administer 5 drops under the tongue whenever I feel stress creeping up the back of my neck. This is a bottled flower essence designed to capture the calm as if you've just received flowers. It works!

-Let's face it, aging begins at birth. In order to keep the 3 million cells you get every day well, you need a super anti-oxidant. I love the product called AgelessXtra by Oasis LifeSciences. It comes in 2 oz bottles to take with you and not only can it knock the 'edge' off your hunger, but it is a whole food and can help you to halt the aging process by repairing those new cells at the cellular level. I love it!

www.oasislifesciences.com

HOLISTIC HEALTH CARE PROVIDERS

If you are having trouble following a regimen to improve your health, seek out a holistic health care practitioner to help get you on track. Here are a few whom I know to be fabulous, providing their patients with alternative modalities of treatment:

Dr. Fredrick Burton, M.D.
(Medical Doctor & Alternative Therapy Doctor)
Burton Wellness & Injury Center
1455 City Line Avenue
Wynnewood, PA 19096
610.649.4325
-or-
321 Emmaus Avenue
Allentown, PA
610.791.2453
www.burtonwellnesscenter.com

Dr. William Holder, M.D.
Center for Preventive Medicine
285 N. Beverwyck Road
Parsippany, NJ 07054
973.331.9774

Queen Afua
Heal Thyself Natural Living Center
106 Kingston Avenue
Brooklyn, NY 11213
718.221.HEAL
www.QueenAfuaOnline.com

Karyn Calabrese
Karyn's Inner Beauty Center
1901 S. Halsted
Chicago, IL
312.255.1590
www.KarynRaw.com

Dr. Beverly Nichols, Ph.D. (Herbalist)
Herbal Connection Holistic Spa
4655 S. Martin Luther King Drive – Suite 105
Chicago, IL 60653
Contact: Peggy Rigins
312.401.9557

Dr. Andrea & Dr. Abigail Pennington
The Pennington Institute
8505 Fenton St. – Suite 206
Silver Spring, MD 20910
301.588.PENN
www.PenningtonInstitute.com

Dr. Sebi
2807 La Cienega Ave.
Los Angeles, CA 90034
310.838.2490

Russell Harrison
Russell Herbal Company
7501 Crenshaw Blvd.
Los Angeles, CA 90045
323.751.1461
www.russellherbal.com

WHERE TO GET HELP

National Black Leadership Commission on AIDS, Inc. (BLCA)
105 E. 22nd St.
New York City, NY 10010
212.614.0023
www.nblca.org

BLCA Affiliate Offices:
Albany, NY
Atlanta, GA
Baltimore, MD
Buffalo, NY
Chicago, IL (opening soon)
Cleveland, OH
Detroit, MI
Los Angeles, CA (opening soon)
Rochester, NY
Syracuse, NY

CAPACITY BUILDING PROVIDERS

Black AIDS Institute
Los Angeles, CA
www.blackaids.org

Community Health Outreach Workers
Detroit, MI
www.chowlinks.org

Education, Training & Research
Scotts Valley, CA
www.etr.org

Harm Reduction Coalition
New York, NY
www.harmreduction.org

Jackson State University
Jackson, MS
www.jsums.edu

Metropolitan Interdenominational Church
Nashville, TN
www.metropolitanfrc.com

My Brother's Keeper
Jackson, MS
www.brotherhood.org

National AIDS Education Services for Minorities
Atlanta, GA
www.naesmonline.org

National Minority AIDS Coalition
Washington D.C.
www.nmac.org

National Youth AIDS Coalition
Washington D.C.
www.nyacyouth.org

The Balm In Gilead
New York, NY
www.balmingilead.org

National Black Alcoholism & Addiction Council
Orlando, FL
www.nyacyouth.org

TECHNICAL ASSISTANCE PROVIDERS

Aegis: An HIV/AIDS Website
www.aegis.com

AIDS Treatment News Online
West Hollywood, CA
www.immunet.org/atn

American Red Cross
Washington D.C.
www.redcross.org

Ark of Refuge, Inc.
San Francisco, CA
www.arkofrefuge.org

CDC National Prevention Information Network
Rockville, MD
www.cdcnpin.org

Centers for Disease Control and Prevention
Atlanta, GA
www.cdc.gov

Computerized AIDS Ministries
New York, NY
http://gbgm-umc.org/cam/

Global Health Council
Washington D.C.
www.globalhealth.org

HIV/AIDS Manual for Faith Communities –
National Coalition of Pastors' Spouses
Memphis, TN
HYPERLINK http://www.pastorsspouses.com
www.pastorsspouses.com

HIV Positive.Com
www.hivpositive.com

Health Power
Brooklyn, NY
www.healthpoweronline.com

Health Resources and Services Administration
Rockville, MD
http://hab.hrsa.gov

HIV InSite
San Francisco, CA
http://hivinsite.ucsf.edu/InSite

National Association of People With AIDS
Silver Spring, MD
www.napwa.org

Project Inform
San Francisco, CA
www.projinf.org

SisterLove, Inc.
Atlanta, GA
www.sisterlove.org

The Body: An AIDS and HIV Information Resource
New York, NY
www.thebody.com/aac/aacpage.html

The Elizabeth Glaser Pediatric AIDS Foundation
New York, NY
www.pedaids.org

The Henry J. Kaiser Family Foundation
Menio Park, CA
www.kff.org

The Family Center
New York, NY
www.thefamilycenter.org

The National Institutes of Health
Bethesda, MD
www.nih.gov

U.S. Department of Health and Human Services
Washington, DC
www.hhs.gov

Treatment Action Group
New York, NY
www.aidsinfonyc.org/tag/index.html

UNAIDS (Information about World AIDS Day)
Geneva 27, Switzerland
www.unaids.org

RESEARCH SITES

American Foundation for AIDS Research
New York, NY
www.amfar.org

Gay Men's Health Crisis
New York, NY
www.gmhc.org

MedScape HIV/AIDS
New York, NY
http://HIV.medscape.com/Home/Topics/AIDS/AIDS.html

RESOURCES

Housing Works
New York
www.housingworks.org

LAMBDA Legal Defense and Education Fund
New York, NY
www.lambdalegal.org

National Catholic AIDS Network
Chicago, IL
www.ncan.org

News About AIDS for the Lutheran Church Missouri Synod Mira
Loma, CA
http://www.planetgary.net/alert/index.html

New York AIDS Coalition
New York, NY
www.nyaidscoalition.org

Project Inform Women's Treatment Issues Site
San Francisco, CA
http://www.projinf.org/pub/ww_index.html

Religion & AIDS Resources
New York, NY
www.thebody.com/religion.html

ON-LINE NEWS LETTERS

News RX
Atlanta, GA
www.newsfile.com/la.html

POZ Magazine
New York, NY
www.POZ.com

LAJOYCE BROOKSHIRE

FAITH UNDER FIRE
Betrayed by a Thing Called Love

WEB OF DECEPTION

SOUL FOOD

Ask LaJoyce Brookshire who she is and quickly she'll tell you she's, "God's Girl!" As author of the novel *Soul Food,* she is the first African American to novelize a major motion picture. She was chosen by HarperCollins Publishing to write the novelization from the movie's script on the strength of her first novel, a suspense drama titled *Web of Deception.* Due to LaJoyce putting to use her marketing and publicity expertise, *Soul Food* has out sold every movie tie-in book ever written.

With *FAITH UNDER FIRE: Betrayed by a Thing Called Love,* LaJoyce takes a pause from fiction and breaks a ten-year silence as she shares the true-life account of her ex-husband marrying her knowing he had AIDS. She has also been a contributing essayist in the books *SOULS OF MY SISTERS: Black Women Break Their Silence, Tell Their Stories, and Heal Their Spirits* and *GHETTOver GIRLS.*

In her many lectures and interviews, LaJoyce covers how to take a book from concept-to computer-to-contract, as well as her experience as an entertainment publicist who has worked with the Queen of Soul Aretha Franklin, Sean "Puffy" Combs, Whitney Houston and Kenny

G., to name a few; and how to break into the genres of publishing and entertainment.

LaJoyce is an ordained minister, a Doctor of Naturopathy, Minister of Health and Master Herbalist; a Certified Group Fitness Instructor; an avid lover of African Dance, and an advocate for literacy and abstinence.

She resides in the Poconos with her husband, childhood sweetheart Gus, daughter Brooke and dogs Rambo, Phoenix and Lexi.